The Global Economic Reset

"The Day America Loses the World Reserve Currency"

By

Fabian Calvo

The New America

Preface

The world in which we live and operate is on the verge of a monumental change. Nations will have their economies completely reset, wars will change the borders of the world, and democracies will rise and fall, many replaced by state run economies with the potential for little economic freedom. In fact, much of these unfortunate scenarios are already underway. Whether it's the Russia Ukraine crisis in the spring of 2014, the potential civil war emerging in the Middle East or the revolutions sweeping places like Venezuela and Thailand...this fundamental change will be ushered in by what I have come to refer to as "The Global Economic Reset", that is, a reset with the ability to unleash a wave of devastation for the unsuspecting masses. Masses that have been programmed with a healthy dose of "bread and circuses" and are completely unsuspecting of the lengths that those who control the global financial system will take in order to centrally plan their economic dystopia.

A mere desire to overcome these great challenges, however, will not lead to success in this new post Global Economic Reset landscape. America's multi-bubble economy has grown massively since the last crash of 2008 to be saved in its current form. Central planners have inflated over half a dozen bubbles, ranging from the government debt bubble and bond bubble to the student debt bubble and derivative bubble.

We are also witnessing the J.O.B. paradigm (Just over Broke) coming to an end and with it the idea of Job security, a luxury once afforded to our parents and grandparents. The government debt bubble, the derivative bubble, the unfunded liabilities and student debt bubble are all interconnected and really revolve around the largest bubble of all, the U.S. Dollar Bubble. When this latter bubble blows, the global economic reset will usher in a new age for the world and the global financial system.

During the cold war the world learned of a new term called MAD, which stands for Mutually Assured Destruction. This was true of the vast nuclear warhead arsenal held by both the then named Soviet Union and the United States. Today those arsenals still exist, as does the idea of MAD. If America launched a nuclear attack against the Russians, those warheads would hit Moscow within 45 minutes of launch. The Russian response would be to fire multiple warheads from submarines positioned off the western and eastern coasts of the U.S., striking major U.S. cities and military bases, assuring the destruction of both countries. This same scenario is now a reality with the economies of the 21st century. The world has become a place of cooperation and conflict alike, just like life on earth utilizes vast sprawling networks of diverse intelligently designed creations to provide for every beings individual needs. Thereby solutions naturally emerge for all sorts of problems that present themselves within our world, and within man himself. In financial markets this concept is often summarized as the "silent hand of the market" a concept originally coined by Scottish economist Adam Smith in the late 1700's.

Humanity is no exception to the rule of interconnectedness. 5,000 years of recorded human history has shown us that despite the exception of a few rare periods of real liberty, which appear almost like a blip on the radar screen of history, tyranny and slavery of the human race has been commonplace. For example, throughout much of the history of Europe individuals would have reported to the king, queen, or feudal lord to receive our fiefs, or payments, for work completed upon our assigned lot. (Hence the term, "one's lot in life") So too, are many people today still reporting to their local feudal lord, but today our local fiefs come from the latest government program, the Ponzi scheme-style social security office or from our employer as many still struggle to break free from the wickedness of being a wage slave. For what does our government or employer require from us to issue such payments? To receive welfare from the state, it requires nothing more than an allegiance to the government, a "go along to get along" attitude or to agree on bipartisanship, as the mainstream media would say and lastly a commitment to find base level employment in some cases by joining the other worker drones that trade their time for fiat currency In addition to these requirements the modern system requires the peasantry to occupy themselves during the day, although in modern society there is less of an emphasis on keeping serfs productive due to television. Television is the most powerful behavioral modification device of all time. It is an extension of the Roman bread and circuses that Caesar so loved to host as he quietly sought to fundamentally alter the Roman republic towards a dictatorship, which eventually led to a bloody civil war in Rome. When it comes to TV, there is a reason the term "programming" is used. To control the peasantry the system uses the modern day equivalent of bread and circuses with TV programming. Whether it is the NFL, Fox News, or American Idol, the six major media companies that control 80% plus of all TV and print media have been tasked with the operation of orchestrating the modern day gladiatorial events. These six major companies are all controlled and financed by the real power brokers of our society, the Wall Street and London mega banks like JP Morgan Chase, CITI, Goldman Sacs, Morgan Stanley, and Wells Fargo. It is evident there is really no separation of power when you get to this level of the game, it all seems to revert back to the good old boys club.

One of the most profound commentaries on the subject of TV programming comes from Neil Postman, in his groundbreaking work, *Amusing Ourselves to Death*.

> *"Television is our culture's principal mode of knowing about itself. Therefore -- and this is the critical point -- how television stages the world becomes the model for how the world is properly to be staged. It is not merely that on the television screen entertainment is the metaphor for all discourse. It is that*

off the screen the same metaphor prevails." (Postman, Amusing Ourselves to Death: Public Discourse in the Age of Show Business)

Sadly, the majority of people in the world today have been programmed as children to in some way serve the system or behave in a way that continues to feed the beast of big government and the power elite. People buy into the fiat currency model, they trust in the fractional reserve banking system, they rack up hundreds of thousands of dollars in debt at college thinking it will land them a higher paying J.O.B, the list can continue for some time. Probably the most sinister type of programming teaches the masses that any big problem is impossible for the individual to handle and therefore the benevolent state must nurture and care for its people through tax payer funded bailouts, bail-ins, and a host of other central planning measures to make everything better.

Think of the many nanny state programs in effect today. Almost all of these programs are used by the state as a creative way to tax or steal more wealth from the people. Without exception these measures are passed under the guise of the state just wants to keep you safe. The best example is probably the red light cameras. Forget about the fact that they have dramatically increased rear end collisions while setting up a nationwide spy grid to control the masses, the state has been successful in implementing the setup of these cameras around the country under the guise of fighting terrorism while preventing dangerous drivers that may speed through a yellow light. The truth is, all of these nanny state programs that the useful idiots usually support are simply a means to raise money for the bankrupt state while gaining more control for the masses it promises to keep safe.

Another major programmed belief perpetuated by government is the idea that all that is really required of you to be a citizen is the ability to consume, an idea used as a psychological buffer to prevent any meaningful reforms or restorations back to a free humanity from taking place. To use a modern example, those who have seen the south park movie might be familiar with operation human shield. Operation human shield required a certain unlucky group of soldiers to be strapped to the outside of tanks as a form of armor previous to the attack. If we look at what is happening today, this is actually pretty close to the reality, albeit in a psychological sense. The central planning authoritarians or what nature refers to as the Alpha predators of our species have insulated themselves from possible harm by using the unintelligible masses as a human shield to prevent any meaningful reforms from taking place. These are the useful idiots who are eager and often times desperate for government to guide them, and to make their life into some form of glowing utopia, that will never exist.

Throughout history the masses are promised gleaming digital utopias, as recounted all too well by the likes of Aldus Huxley, George Orwell, and Phillip K. Dick all the while subconsciously witnessing the horrors and atrocities produced by their own acquisitiveness. A lifetime spent in self-flagellation for the vices that were so easily avoided in times past, yet reinforcement of subconscious programming makes breaking free of this tangled web increasing difficult; albeit more rewarding than ever. Breaking free from the J.O.B. paradigm can be one of the most liberating things an individual can do in life, as well as one of the most powerful weapons in our struggle against the authoritarians.

Yet not all are useful idiots, thank God. There are many that recognize the evil at hand and understand that self-reliance is needed more than ever before. For if we truly seek freedom, we must by default assume the mantle of complete and utter personal responsibility in our life. Those who are smarter than the average grunt are (generally speaking) easily co-opted through money, drugs, sex, or promises of power. Not to mention good old fashioned blackmail. These are the types of controls that the state employs to keep people in the media, government, and overall establishment passive, tranquil, and out of their business, and methods of which the common moral man should always guard against. For if you can't even control yourself, who else can you trust to control you?

So now we find ourselves toe to toe with the global economic system and fast approaching economic reset of this system. Atlas is shrugging before our very eyes, much to the chagrin of the benevolent benefactor's within our society. If we can somehow awaken our fellow brothers and sister by setting powerful examples of what self-reliance can bring, and let the natural equilibriums of the universe, or free hand of the market, bring us back into balance, perhaps there is hope for us yet.

Withstanding the blights of central planners, specifics, and castles made of sand, we certainly have our hands full. The western world might surprise itself yet, and ascend back up to its proper place in the cosmos while breaking the chains of bondage shackled upon its people by the authoritarian central planners who seek to enslave humanity once again. At the very least we should strive to elevate ourselves back to an age of mass sanity. People may live to see a day in which every being born in this world can enjoy the right to live in an economic system that is founded upon principals of equal justice, truly free market capitalism, and an end to the central banking crony capitalism that has defined the last hundreds years in America; thereby leaving an economic system that rewards ingenuity, real production and value.

Global economic resets are nothing new. They have happened many times in the past but never to a society as programmed, unsuspecting and generally spoiled as is America today. The forces pushing for this reset understands that time is not on their side. As millions of more Westerners continue to awaken to their financial crimes and treason we can eventually stop them. Evil seeks ignorance to breed and grow and that is exactly what is happening today. Close to a majority in America alone have lost all notions of their inner beauty and unique abilities.

These unique abilities, if acted upon, would make the role of the state in their life almost useless and by default result in the individual truly being the master of their destiny. This book hopes to expose the truth of the coming global economic reset, to set forward a path where everyday people can prepare themselves for the wickedness that comes this way and most importantly find their true inner power in their personal journey to what the creator wants for us all, to become self-reliant while sharing our unique abilities with the world.

1 History of the World Reserve Currency

To begin to tell a story as wild as the reality of the 21st century banking practices; one must first find refuge within the annals of history. History is the age-old cyclical teacher that cannot lie, at least beyond the capacity of kings to concoct fables. These fables generally recount the greatness of the historical victor's lineage, and the empires that were built on top of the sacrifices of the deceased. While many truths of history may remain hidden, the overall circumstantial evidence of economic boom and bust cycles has been thoroughly documented, and should be reckoned with as a signpost for the future development of our species. For within the past, lies the blueprint towards a brighter future.

The history of global trade within the Western world can be traced back towards the Roman Empire. All roads lead to Rome as they say. The Romans did not mince words with civilizations. It was either pay tribute to them, or be conquered; and so began the western history of a global reserve currency. If you were not using the Roman Denarius to conduct your transactions, you were on a short list, essentially waiting to be dominated. Along with that, the Denarius was also one of the first historical examples of devaluation and hyperinflation due to mass production.

> *"The dominance of the Roman-issued coins was brought to an end as the long cycle of inflation that characterized the economy of the Roman Empire from the first century C.E. through the early fourth century led to a continuous devaluation of the Roman-issued currency, causing it to become increasingly less accepted outside the Roman Empire. Ultimately, the Denarius became valued according to its weight rather than its imputed "face value," trading more as a commodity than a currency outside the Roman Empire and making way for the Byzantine Empire's heavy gold solidus coin to become the dominant currency in international trade in the sixth century. (Zero Hedge, 2014)*

Soon after the Roman hyperinflation scenario, the Byzantine Empire had taken over, retaining the title of world reserve currency status for almost 800 years. During that time the Solidus was the preferred method of currency within the world, dominating longer than even the Roman system had. Although there were definitely savings and loans systems during these time periods, it was nothing nearly as complex as the systems that have been enacted today. Individuals could store their gold or silver in a bank and in return be issued paper money which was back by their deposit. More importantly one must consider the honesty in this system. Keep in mind the fact that in those days if you didn't pay someone back, it was generally punishable by death depending on the amounts involved, so there was a lot less room for chicanery within the system. Obviously if you were born into the elite banking caste you probably had a good amount more wiggle room but overall people took crime deadly serious. If you screwed someone over you were liable to be hunted down and killed.

To be clear, the global reserve currency can be defined as the dominant currency that other countries depend upon to gauge the value of their own currencies--allowing for international standardization, which equates to easier trade. Without much exception global reserve currency status is generally retained by the current military superpower of the age. Although to a lesser extent it also seems to hinge upon other factors such as transportation capabilities of the issuing empire (Roman roads, British Ships, American Airplanes etc.), and the weight or amount of precious metals within the minted coins, what many refer to as "real" money. Take the British Pound for example, which was the world reserve currency for over 150 years and at its inception was backed by one pound of silver, hence the name. Its world reserve currency status was not due to the backing of silver alone; Britain at the time had a vast naval military might, sophisticated banking system, and vast trading networks. Pre-Internet and UPS, people actually had to go and put things on ships via chartered merchants in order to acquire wares from other parts of the world. Britain's massive navy was the main reason they were able to retain financial dominance during that period, because protecting the cargo from pirates, and military attack was essential for economic security during those times. They were the world's leading importers for most of the 1800's which lead to favorable exchange rates for those countries choosing to do business in the British Pound Sterling.

> *"It was only when national central banks and treasuries began holding gold as reserves, beginning in the 19th century, that bills and interest-bearing deposit claims could be substituted for gold also began to be held as reserves. This development coincided with the rise of Great Britain as the leading exporter of manufactured goods and services and the largest importer of*

food and industrial raw materials. Between the early 1860s and the outbreak of World War I in 1914, some 60 percent of the world's trade was invoiced in British pounds sterling.

As U.K. banks expanded their overseas business, propelled by innovations in communications technology such as the telegraph, the British Pound was increasingly used as a currency of denomination for commercial transactions between non-U.K. residents—that is, the pound sterling became a more international currency. This role for the pound was further enhanced by London's emergence as the world's leading shipper and insurer of traded goods and as a center for organized commodities markets, as well as by the growing amount of British foreign investment, of which a large share was in the form of long-term securities denominated in pounds sterling." (Zero Hedge, 2014)

It is also important to note that this is around the same time physical gold coinage stopped being used again, in lieu of gold backed and non-gold backed paper currency the latter leading to ugly bouts of hyperinflation throughout many parts of Europe that implemented this experiment with fiat currency. Comparatively speaking, the American dollar is the new kid on the block, and coming eminently close to losing its peak spot due to overwhelmingly unstable fiscal policies and irrational military engagements within the past several decades. Our role as the military aggressor has not helped our reserve currency relations with China or Russia much. Both of these countries use dollars to purchase many other goods worldwide (even if they don't purchase much from us), most notably oil which we will talk more about in Chapter 3. It would seem obvious that no sovereign country wants to store their wealth in a nation which might attack them in the future.

Due to the corporate multi-billion dollar oil and narcotics agendas the west has made it clear that the domination and whoring out of the Middle East in the name of oil, and illicit drug trade is priority number one. The wars waged in the Middle East have created a massive treasure trove for the 21st century military industrial complex, and have catapulted the region into complete turmoil. The volume of heroine coming out of Afghanistan is staggering...

"Drug trafficking is the largest global commodity in profits after the oil and arms trade, consequently, "immediately following

the October 2001 invasion opium markets were restored. Opium prices spiraled. By early 2002, the domestic price of opium in Afghanistan (in dollars/kg) was almost 10 times higher than in 2000." The Anglo-American invasion of Afghanistan successfully restored the drug trade. The Guardian recently reported that, *"In 2007 Afghanistan had more land growing drugs than Colombia, Bolivia and Peru combined."* (Geo Political Monitor, 2014)

If you dig a little deeper, you will realize that the West's policy of strategic control of the Middle East is nothing new.

"From the middle of last century Washington's foreign policy priority in the Middle East was to establish U.S. control over what the State Department described as "a stupendous source of strategic power and one of the great material prizes in world history", namely the region's vast reserves of crude oil. Middle Eastern oil was regarded in Washington as "probably the richest economic prize in the world in the field of foreign investment", in what President Eisenhower described as the most "strategically important area in the world".

"Control could be most easily maintained via a number of despotic feudal oligarchies in the Gulf which ensured the extraordinary wealth of the region would be shared between a small number of ruling families and US oil companies, rather than European commercial competitors or the population of these states. Until recently the US has not required the oil for itself though it needed to ensure that the oil price stayed within a desirable range or band - not too low for profit making or too high to discourage consumption and induce inflation. A side benefit of this control over such a vital industrial resource is the influence it gives the US over economic development in rival countries such as Japan." (Oil Control, 2014)

One of the most interesting points within this whole debate is the fact that many countries are insanely willing to try untested, highly unstable models, in the name of finding a magic bullet to finance. All it takes is some young economic hotshot and it seems like governments of the 1700-1800's were willing to try just about anything and take a roll of the dice on issuing a new paper currency. Perhaps they were all hoping to eventually become the world reserve currency as well, who's to say? You could almost equate it to opening a new kind of business, without proper planning the seed money will be squandered in a few months, and the whole project will go bust. The accounts of economists making up new economic models out of thin air are nothing new. This is probably the best description of Keynesian economics, the economic school of thought that has come to define the Western world. These hair brain schemes generally all end the same, with every single example resulting in a debasement of the currency and a massive distortion of the markets. During the 1700's the French issued many different types of currency, each one more hyper-inflated than the next. It was a sad and strange cycle that the country went through. The following article from the Ludwig Von Mises Institute of Economics goes a long way towards solving the conundrum. It reveals the sad bout of French hyperinflation during the late 1700s; an event that took place only 50 years after another failed currency experiment had resulted in the same financial madness. As you read notice how similar it sounds to the reasoning the central planners give for the modern day money printing taking place in America known has Q.E., Quantitative Easing.

"Many Frenchman soon became eternal optimists claiming that inflation was prosperity, like the drunk forgetting the inevitable hangover. Although every new issuance initially boosted

economic activity, the improved business conditions became shorter and shorter after each new issuance. Commercial activity soon became spasmodic: one manufacturer after another closed shop. Money was losing its store-of-value function, making business decisions extremely difficult in an environment of uncertainty. Foreigners were blamed and heavy taxes were levied against foreign goods. The great manufacturing centers of Normandy closed down and the rest of France speedily followed, throwing vast numbers of workers into bread lines. The collapse of manufacturing and commerce was quick, and occurred only a few months after the second issuance of assignats and followed the same path as Austria, Russia, America, and all other countries that had previously tried to gain prosperity on a mountain of paper."- Frank Hollenbeck

Sadly it would seem that the French were gluttons for punishment, and these hyperinflationary bust cycles were created in order to consolidate wealth within the regions, and to assume complete control when the system went bust. It's a sad fact that during these large booms and busts, the financiers are generally the only ones to make out like bandits, while the common unsuspecting working class usually gets hosed. Both corrupt politicians and elitists love fiat currency, although the currency breeds an untold amount of instability, it still seems to suit those bureaucrats who know how to work the angles and use the loopholes to get ahead. As the saying goes, there is really nothing new under the sun. John Locke, the French pioneering economist led one of the biggest fiat disasters of all time early in the 1700's in which the printing of currency got way out of hand, yet somehow 50 years later, France tried the exact same thing again. All these fiat currencies are really beneficial for those trying to orchestrate a mass transfer of wealth, or outright highway robbery. Mr. Hollenbeck goes on to state:

> *"Everything was enormously inflated in price except the wages for labor. As manufacturers closed, wages collapsed. Those who did not have the means, foresight, or skill to transfer their worthless paper into real assets were driven into poverty. By 1797, most of the currency was in the hands of the working class and the poor. The entire episode was a massive transfer of real wealth from the poor to the rich, similar to what we are experiencing in Western societies today.*

The French government tried to issue a new currency called the mandate, but by May 1797 both currencies were virtually worthless. Once the dike was broken, the money poured through and the currency was swollen beyond control. As Voltaire once said, "Paper money eventually returns to its intrinsic value — zero." In France, it took nearly 40 years to bring capital, industry, commerce, and credit back up to the level attained in 1789."

The question remains, what will happen in America when this exact scenario unfolds? We will discuss these possible scenarios in Chapter 7. It is inevitable that it will be much worse since we are in control of a much bigger chunk of the world economy. All we can surmise is that the banking elite always operate under the motto of problem, reaction, solution. They create the problem, they frame the public reaction with the media, and they create the solution that leads to their desired means. The dumbed-down populations' of the world had little chance of decoding this monarchical mystery; until now that is. We finally live in an age where all of the tactics of the oppressors of the world systems are being revealed, and the future of the population will be much better off as a result.

These long-term shifts in dominant world currency never occur by the luck of the draw, as we may be lead to believe. As we will discover in later chapters, there are no accidents when it comes to world finance. In regards to the control of the global money supply, nothing is left to chance. Currencies can be supported through brute force, but in recent history the velvet glove has been used instead. The human penchant for greed in certain people can explain this all too easily. If someone came to you and said that you could have the printing press to create money out of thin air, would you turn it down? Most people might not, even if it meant destroying the wealth of the producers while playing divide and conquer with the most naïve sections of the population. The human ego is quite capable of inventing some fanciful stories in order to justify deplorable actions; history has proven this time and time again. Luckily for us, evil contains within it, the seeds of its very destruction.

Breaking money theory down into a base level, it would make sense that if you want to put your money somewhere, you want to make sure that that place is either,

A. Very secure, and thieves can't easily steal it.

Or

B. Well outside of the purview of any potential thieves and looters.

Hence, you had the common sense approach of pirates who buried their treasure on deserted islands, or buried it in non-descript locales for later retrieval. If we think about currency in these base level contexts, we can quickly decode the psychological underpinnings of the global money supply.

We must also ask why the banking world is made to sound ultra-complex, utilizing words like quantitative easing, M3 money supply and derivatives to confuse and disinterest the masses who are most affected by these insane monetary policies. There is no doubt that this, too, is a purposeful plan. When you make things too confusing for the general populace to understand, then you can control them through their ignorance. They also make the history of money seem to be a dry and boring subject, when you can rest assured it is anything but. The old stereotypical image of the miserable banker sitting behind a calculator needs to be updated. A more accurate depiction of the top elite bankers would be a conniving trust fund baby, with sociopathic and narcissistic tendencies. We are dealing with serious "creeple" here, seriously psycho "creeple". They seem to have an insatiable urge for financial domination. As the Buddha said… "If you give a man a mountain of gold, he will ask for another."

The world reserve currencies have been a hotly contested battle for eons. It has also been the cause of more wars than you can shake a stick at, so why wouldn't we consider a massive banking shift as the prime suspect leading to most of the current strife in the world today. Usury, or the ability to lend money at interest, was forbidden for hundreds of years due to the economic debauchery that would ensue. Who banned Usury you might ask? Well, consider that both the Romans, and the Catholic Church alike, considered it a reprehensible practice.

> *"Plato (Laws, v. 742) and Aristotle (Politics, I, x, xi) considered interest as contrary to the nature of things; Aristophanes expressed his disapproval of it, in the "Clouds" (1283 sq.); Cato condemned it (see Cicero, "De officiis, II, xxv), comparing it to homicide, as also did Seneca (De beneficiis, VII, x) and Plutarch in his treatise against incurring debts. So much for Greek and Roman writers, who, it is true, knew little of economic science.*

Aristotle disapproved of the money trader's profit; and the ruinous rates at which money was lent explain his severity. On the other hand, the Roman and Greek laws while considering the loan for consumption, as a contract gratuitous in principle, allowed a clause, stipulating for the payment of interest, to be added to the bond. The Law of the Twelve Tables allowed only unciarium fenus, probably one-twelfth of the capital, or 8.33 per cent. A plebiscitum (a Roman decree) went so far as to forbid all interest whatsoever, but, at a later period, the Roman law allowed interest at 1 per cent monthly, or 12 per cent per annum. Justinian lay down as a general rule that this maximum should be reduced by half. No absolute prohibition can be found in the Old Testament; at most, Exodus 22:25, and Deuteronomy 23:19-20, forbid the taking of interest by one Jew from another."

It wasn't until the 1600s that many of the Usury laws were lifted for Christians, although the Jewish community had generally been immune to such laws, highlighting their involvement within the high levels of banking worldwide. Actually, one can trace the ban on usury all the way back to the Old Testament, which leads us to a study of economic prehistory which may be pursued at a later date. If you are going to untangle a mystery, you must first strike at the root. A difficult task when those roots are thousands of years old. It is still very interesting to note, as it is the progenitor to a world reserve currency ever being invented.

> *"It is a curious fact that for a long time impunity in such matters was granted to Jews. The Fourth Council of the Lateran (1215), only forbids them to exact excessive interest. Urban III and St. Louis in twenty-three of his regulations extended the prohibition to the Jews. With the exception of the Fourth Council of the Lateran, we know of no canon law which takes into consideration the question of moderate interest; and canon law nowhere states distinctly that interest is, under any circumstances whatsoever, contrary to justice." -Vermeersch, A. (New Advent, 2014)*

As any modern economist would explain, two of the main driving forces behind economics are fear and scarcity. Therefore the more afraid the people are, the less they will spend their money, and the less people spend their money, the more scarce real prosperity becomes. Within this model we find the ultimatum handed down to us by the creators of the controlled world currencies of the new millennium. You can either acquiesce to the presence of a new controlled digital all world currency, or be forced to drift among the never-regions of bartering. Additionally, we could abandon their hellish systems of control and pioneer our own economic system going forward. We can create an economic system free of monopolized control and the gangster-style extortion of wealth by the central banks of the world. Fiat currency is an outdated model which will eventually make the old, precious metals, new again, as well as the rise of crypto currencies which are completely decentralized and out of the control of the power hungry authoritarians. America was founded on just such principles, so if it happened once, it can happen again.

2 The Reign of the Dollar

The dollar originally rose to prominence on the coat tails of World War Two. Although the founding fathers of the United States had encouraged trade, they also warned against foreign entanglements. This creates the question of what their position would have been on issues such as becoming the global reserve currency (aka bank of the world). The conjecture one would formulate from all of the writings seems to be that the founders that cherished smaller government would have certainly opposed such measures. This is one of the most famous Jeffersonian quotations to denote such sentiments.

"Thomas Jefferson wrote in 1825 to William Branch Giles of "a vast accession of strength from their younger recruits, who, having nothing in them of the feelings or principles of '76, now look to a single and splendid government of an aristocracy, founded on banking institutions, and moneyed corporations under the guise and cloak of their favored branches of manufactures, commerce and navigation, riding and ruling over the plundered ploughman and beggared yeomanry." -Thomas Jefferson

Washington was no fan either. George Washington, in letter to J. Bowen, Rhode Island, Jan. 9, 1787:

"Paper money has had the effect in your state that it will ever have, to ruin commerce, oppress the honest, and open the door to every species of fraud and injustice."

Roosevelt also knew something was askew:

"In a letter to Edward M. House (President Wilson's closest aide), dated November 23, 1933, Franklin D. Roosevelt said: "The real truth of the matter is, and you and I know, that a financial element in the large centers has owned the government of the U.S. since the days of Andrew Jackson."

Although Jefferson died dead broke, one must admire his idealism and his respect for the sovereignty of our nation's fiscal affairs. Ultimately he realized the real dangers of a naïve population to get screwed over by a decedent fiat system. He knew that without fiscal autonomy, real freedom wasn't going to exist. Sadly this perennial advice fell upon dead ears, perhaps even literally. His advice was falling on the dead ears of those killed by the quickly emerging United States banking cabal, as many Americans were assassinated while protecting the right to sound currency. Although the most ardent opponent of central banking in the United States had to have been Andrew Jackson, Jackson himself survived two well-documented assassination attempts. The following is a statement from a letter to congress explaining why he vetoed the legislation trying to establish a central bank of the United States.

"In another of its bearings this provision is fraught with danger. Of the twenty-five directors of this bank five are chosen by the Government and twenty by the citizen stockholders. From all voice in these elections the foreign stockholders are excluded by the charter. In proportion, therefore, as the stock is transferred to foreign holders the extent of suffrage in the choice of directors is curtailed. Already almost a third of the stock is in foreign hands and not represented in elections. It is constantly passing out of the country, and this act will accelerate its departure. The entire control of the institution would necessarily fall into the hands of a few citizen stockholders, and the ease with which the object would be accomplished would be a temptation to designing men to secure that control in their own hands by monopolizing the remaining stock. There is danger that a president and directors would then be able to elect themselves from year to year, and without responsibility or control manage the whole concerns of the bank during the existence of its charter. It is easy to conceive that great evils to our country and its institutions millet flow from such a

concentration of power in the hands of a few men irresponsible to the people." (The Money Masters, 2014)

This passage clearly summarizes the real problem with the world reserve currency status, and relates the clear and present dangers present within these powerful currency control mechanisms. Jackson took great umbrage to the fact that the United States would have its hand in some form on the mutilated banking monarchy, and was willing to die to prevent it. Preventing the fiscal tyranny was the pride of his legacy, as he noted within his memoirs.

"It is to be regretted that the rich and powerful too often bend the acts of government to their selfish purposes. Distinctions in society will always exist under every just government. Equality of talents, of education, or of wealth cannot be produced by human institutions. In the full enjoyment of the gifts of Heaven and the fruits of superior industry, economy, and virtue, every man is equally entitled to protection by law; but when the laws undertake to add to these natural and just advantages artificial distinctions, to grant titles, gratuities, and exclusive privileges, to make the rich richer and the potent more powerful, the

humble members of society — the farmers, mechanics, and laborers — who have neither the time nor the means of securing like favors to themselves, have a right to complain of the injustice of their government. There are no necessary evils in government. Its evils exist only in its abuses. If it would confine itself to equal protection, and, as Heaven does its rains, shower its favors alike on the high and the low, the rich and the poor, it would be an unqualified blessing." (Jackson, 1832)

He knew that if America went down the road of printed fiat money, there would be no limits to the amount of corruption such a system could breed. Sadly America had already been through this whole gambit before during the American Revolution, with the fiat Continental currency.

The History of Inflation in America

The Continental was a currency printed from 1775-1781 in the 13 colonies to finance the Revolutionary War—understanding the Continental is crucial if you want to understand the historical precedents of U.S .dollar policy. America had already effectively screwed itself economically during the time of the revolutionary and civil wars through the printing of the fiat money. These inflationary bouts pale in comparison to the earlier discussed French hyperinflation where monthly inflation peaked at 143%, yet the results were equally devastating. Even at the time, the founders knew that the printing of a fiat currency was a bad plan, yet they had no other choice. It was a do or die scenario, as they needed a serious payment mechanism to create a warfare budget, as well as money to pay the veterans that had fought for Washington.

> *"Ironically, the Revolutionary War demonstrated the weaknesses of "currency financing" in a really major period of need. First, the Continental Congress issued paper with no ability to redeem the notes. The colonies had been adamant that the central government not share their taxing power. By the end of 1776, the Congress had printed $25,000,000 in continental currency, very close to the limit that the entire economy could absorb, not counting the fact that each individual state was also printing money.*

Their choice was to continue printing or abandon the war —
"any quantity of brown paper" would serve. That the
"continental dollar" devalued disastrously is thus not surprising.

The individual colonies didn't fare much better since they found
it necessary to print far more paper, just to keep up with the war
effort, than they could expect to redeem in any reasonable
period of time. George Washington, in his ledger book, lists costs
in both dollars and in "lawful money", which were colonial
pounds according to the official depreciation scale adopted by
Congress.

The worst fears of the aristocrats and merchants came true.
They concluded that the problems were because the "policy of
government is dictated by the multitude". Many left outright
and many more, when Britain lost the war, chose to move to
England or to other English colonies. They completely missed the
fact that the problems were largely beyond the control of
Congress. Although true to their prejudices, they missed the
opportunity to be part of the beginning of the greatest economy
the world has ever seen." –James E. Newell

The Continental was plagued with problems from the outset, as its whole fiscal structure was based upon projected tax revenues. Basically it equated to a fancy IOU, and eventually the system would succumb to hyperinflation. This happened for two reasons, first of which was counterfeiting. As time drew on, other people were able to recreate the currency with newer advances in printing, and minting technologies. The second reason was due to a vast overprinting of the currency, a familiar scenario of most historical hyperinflation instances. The Continental eventually collapsed and its failed experiment prompted the founders to include the gold and silver clause in the Constitution which prevented states from issuing bills of credit or make anything but gold and silver coin a tender in the payment of debts.

America's second hyperinflation episode took place with the South during the Civil War. The following passage describes what happened to the economy when hyperinflation had fully taken effect post-civil war.

"From October of 1861 to March of 1864 the commodity price index raised an average rate of 10 percent per month. When the Civil War ended in April 1865 the cost of living in the South was

92 times what it was before the war started. This inflation was obviously caused by the expansion of the money supply. The role of the money supply in establishing the price level is confirmed even more strongly by the results of an attempt to curb the growth of the money supply in 1864.

In February the Confederate Congress decreed a currency reform. All bills greater than five dollars were to be converted into bonds paying 4 percent interest. All bills not converted by April would be exchanged for a new issue at a ratio of 2 for 3. Prior to the reform people spent wildly and drove prices up 23 percent in one month. But, by May 1864, the reform had been completed and the stock of money was reduced by one third. The general price index declined. Eugene Lerner, an economist who studied this inflation, commented on this result:

This price decline took place in spite of invading Union armies, the impending military defeat, reduction of foreign trade, the disorganized government, and the low morale of the Confederate army. Reducing the stocks of money had a more significant effect on prices than these powerful forces.

The increase in the money supply came as a result of the Confederacy's inability to collect funds through taxes. Only 5 percent of its expenditures were covered by taxes. Initially the Confederate government tried to borrow extensively. This failed because the planters had funds only after the fall harvest, but the war started in April. The war interfered with the harvest and export of the cotton crop so the planters were asking the government for help instead of loaning it funds. Consequently less than 30 percent of the funds for the Confederacy came from bonds. Thus, the Confederate government saw printing money as an unavoidable method for financing the war. The Confederate Congress was reluctant to use this measure and stated in the act, which authorized the printing of money that it was "not to exceed at any one time one million of dollars."
Actually 1500 times this amount was printed.

The printing of such large sums created a major problem. Paper engravers and printers were hard to find. In desperation, the Secretary of the Treasury recommended that counterfeit money be utilized. Anyone holding a counterfeit bill was supposed to exchange it for a government bond and the government would stamp it "valid" and spend it."

This fiscal model led to a tremendous loss of wealth and untold suffering for middle class and poor in the South. The wealthy plantation owners mostly took payments in only gold and silver, so they saw their wealth preserved while once again the unsuspecting masses got punished. This whole episode happened a mere 100-150 years ago; yet despite these lessons of the economic past, an even more unstable system has been installed today. It seems as though the winds of fate have blown us in a vastly different direction than the fiscally sustainable model set forth by Andrew Jackson, and instead were headed straight into the ditch. The global power brokers are running little more than an economic whorehouse, yet somehow the United States dollar seems to have some demand left. Despite being beat up and abused for over a century now, they still have their prize pony with which to continue their plan for global domination. Although America initially thrived early with these fiat currency experiments it was very short lived. Ultimately greed, war, and strife reared their ugly heads and without a currency backed by something of real value to rely upon; in the post-civil war South this lesson was realized as many had lost a vast majority of their savings and wealth. Losing everything you own is pretty harsh in itself, but when you couple it with the fact that much of the south had been virtually burned to the ground, it was especially brutal. These circumstances made for a painfully slow rebuilding effort overall.

> *"The enormous cost of the Confederate war effort took a high toll on the South's economic infrastructure. The direct costs to the Confederacy in human capital, government expenditures, and physical destruction from the war totaled $3.3 billion. By 1865, the Confederate dollar was worthless due to high inflation, and people in the South had to resort to bartering services for goods, or else use scarce Union dollars. With the emancipation of the southern slaves, the entire economy of the South had to be rebuilt." (Berman, 2014)*

Morris Berman goes on to describe how the median income had dropped over 40%.

> *"Over a quarter of Southern white men of military age — meaning the backbone of the South's white workforce — died during the war, leaving countless families destitute. Per capita income for white southerners declined from $125 in 1857 to a*

low of $80 in 1879. By the end of the 19th century and well into the 20th century, the South was locked into a system of poverty." (Berman, 2014)

Another thing to highlight is that fact that during those times people had a much more refined work ethic. Laziness was culturally frowned upon at this point in American history, and for many people, it was a quick way to starve. The American work ethic helped the country bounce back from economic crises much faster than many other countries, historically speaking. In a post U.S. dollar collapse Americans will be dealing with a new breed of entitlement-based Americans, who might not have had to work a hard day's labor in their entire life. The moral of the story remains that where there is discipline, continuity, and fortitude, things prosper and rebuild. Where there are slothfulness, overconfidence, and arrogance there will be decline and eventual collapse.

As an interesting aside, the famous literary giant Ezra Pound was actually one of the first people to break the news of what had happened on Jekyll Island in 1910. This was the meeting in which the banking elite of the day planned out the formation of the Federal

Reserve. In 1950 after being falsely imprisoned in an insane-asylum Mr. Pound commissioned (now conspiracy legend) Eustice Mullins to write the book *Secrets of the Federal Reserve*, which was published in 1954, albeit in a limited release. Pound was quoted as saying the following regarding the formation of the Federal Reserve...

> *"Here are the simple facts of the great betrayal. Wilson and House knew that they were doing something momentous. One cannot fathom men's motives and this pair probably believed in what they were up to. What they did not believe in was representative government. They believed in government by an uncontrolled oligarchy whose acts would only become apparent after an interval so long that the electorate would be forever incapable of being efficient to remedy depredations." (Dr. Ezra Pound, 1950)*

After 10 to 15 years of people starving during the great depression, people were ready to do nearly anything to get the economy up and running again, up to and including warfare. That's how the common dictators operate; first they break your spirit, and then convince you that giving them more control is the answer. At the time, the bankers needed another world war to create demand for their military expenditures, and newly developed war toys, so Germany was conveniently built up to be the psychotic bogeyman of the age. In the years preceding the war companies like Ford, JP Morgan, GM, IBM and others were the reason Germany rose to industrial prominence so quickly.

> "In brief, American companies associated with the Morgan-Rockefeller international investment bankers - not, it should be noted, the vast bulk of independent American industrialists - were intimately related to the growth of Nazi industry... General Motors, Ford, General Electric, DuPont and the handful of U.S. companies intimately involved with the development of Nazi Germany were - except for the Ford Motor Company - controlled by the Wall Street elite - the J. P. Morgan firm, the Rockefeller Chase Bank and to a lesser extent the Warburg Manhattan bank." (Sutto, 2014)

I would venture a guess to say that it's easy to win a war when the enemy is fighting with all of the weapons that you handed them. Whatever the case, after World War 2, America was the golden child worldwide, so everyone pretty much went along with whatever solutions the United States came up with. This quickly set the bankers in motion to create a more sophisticated world reserve currency and in turn giving them even more global control and effectively consolidating their power via worldwide currency manipulation.

This agreement came to be known as the Bretton Woods Agreement, a very devilish system indeed. It was the beginning of America's take over as a world reserve currency, and the demise of its fiscal independence. The general populace had fiercely opposed our involvement in the League of Nations previous to World War 1, as it was viewed as a threat to national sovereignty. Yet after World War 2 had ended, the PR machines of the bankers had been able to effectively spin public opinion into accepting a world governing body. Like most political shenanigans, it ended up being great for short-term economic growth. As any good politician knows, you have to dangle a carrot in order to get people on board with your plans.

To quickly surmise Bretton Woods, it was an agreement that gave the banking cartels major control over the global economic system, also giving The United States the right to issue a world currency.

Previous to Bretton Woods, the English had been the only ones fiscally dominating Europe for the past 100 plus years. The agreement had amounted to little more than a kickback for the American taxpayer. The bankers said... you let go of economic control, and we will give you some pocket change. In the short term Bretton Woods was able to develop a fiscal system that was much more stable worldwide, albeit totally rigged and manipulated.

Many of the causes of World War I originated in the banking system, and on the heels of World War II, there seemed to be moments of sanity occurring amongst at least some of the global populace who were tired of the bloodshed. People knew that a stable financial system could breed a newfound peace for the world while at the same time failing to realize that there would be strings attached. Up until that point the currency system had been way too unstable and had wild swings in global currency valuations. Under the new Bretton Woods system, many of these issues were addressed by restricting the free-floating currency rate system. This had allowed too many people to revalue currencies at a whim, with sometimes-dire consequences for the general populace. The old system used during the seventeenth and eighteenth centuries, relied on totally fixed valuations. That made it difficult to issue loans under lean economic times, to help restart economic development. Neither of these were amazing plans long-term so the United States came in with a different plan.

The United States plan, of a pegged (yet still floating) currency was adopted. Granted the terms of this are a little complex, the detailed effects of the system are succinctly summarized by Benjamin Cohen here:

"As matters turned out, their optimism (in global goodwill money lending) proved utterly Panglossian. Monetary relations after the war were anything but stable, the transitional period anything but brief, the Fund's initial resources anything but sufficient to cope with emerging payment difficulties. Hence after a short burst of activity during its first two years, IMF lending shrank to an extremely small scale for over a decade. Instead, the burden was shifted to the one actor at the time with the financial and economic resources needed to shoulder responsibility for global monetary stabilization - namely, the United States.

Fortunately, for reasons of its own, the United States was not only able but willing to take on that responsibility, in effect assuming the role of global monetary hegemon: money manager of the world. American hegemony was exercised principally in three ways. First, a relatively open market was maintained for imports of foreign goods. Second, a generous flow of long-term loans and grants was initiated, first through the Marshall Plan and other related aid programs, then through the reopened New York capital market. Third, a liberal lending policy was eventually established for provision of shorter-term funds in time of crisis. Since the reserves of most countries were near exhaustion and the Fund's pool of liquidity was manifestly inadequate, the rest of the world was more than willing to accumulate dollars. Given the scarcity of central bank gold outside the United States and limited prospects for new gold production, America became the residual source of global liquidity growth through the deficits in its own balance of payments. Other governments with payment surpluses stabilized their exchange rates by buying dollars. The United States pledged convertibility of its dollars into gold at a fixed price, thus making the greenback a near perfect substitute for

gold." (Cohen, 2014)

Although this system seemed well and good, it most definitely consolidated power in a very eerie and unsettling way. To the point where all countries had to go through the dollar to do pretty much anything, as all of the bigger fiscal deals had to be done in dollars or pounds. This led to a period of major economic dominance for the United States and England that spanned from 1945-1972. These were some of the economic golden years for economic development in America. It's no wonder we enjoyed such a boom cycle during these times, as the whole system was rigged in our favor. I guess this is always how it goes; the banks bring up the masses with a warm and fuzzy economic feeling, just to later take the same group down the road of economic turmoil. All the early Bretton Woods period amounted to was a chef lathering up a pig with butter before the slaughter.

This same economic boom cycle was also rife with drug epidemics, effectively diverting people's attention from real common sense economic issues. If people are partying like drunken sailors, and stoned all day, are they really going to notice that there country is losing fiscal accountability? No of course not, they were too busy dropping out of the system, and who can blame them? When there is no bogeyman left in the closet, who is there left to rebel against besides you? The problem being, if good people don't enter government, bad people will. Yet as of 1971 the jig was up, foreign countries worldwide were beginning to get hip to our economic jive, and started to bail out of the Bretton Woods agreement.

"By 1971, the money supply had increased by 10%. In May 1971, West Germany was the first to leave the Bretton Woods system, unwilling to devalue the Deutsche Mark in order to prop up the dollar. In the following three months, this move strengthened its economy. Simultaneously, the dollar dropped 7.5% against the Deutsche Mark. Other nations began to demand redemption of their dollars for gold. Switzerland redeemed $50 million in July. France acquired $191 million in gold. On August 5, 1971, the United States Congress released a report recommending devaluation of the dollar, in an effort to protect the dollar against "foreign price-gougers". On August 9, 1971, as the dollar dropped in value against European currencies, Switzerland left

the Bretton Woods system. The pressure began to intensify on the United States to leave Bretton Woods."

After this currency withdrawal domino effect started to take place, then President Nixon had a meeting with his economic advisors and the Federal Reserve chairman. During the meeting they decided that in order to shore up the dollar and stabilize things against world exchange rate volatility, he would take the dollar off of the gold standard. This event eventually came to be known as the Nixon Shock. Although the removal of the gold standard is thoroughly disconcerting long-term, shorter term the event was hailed as a massive success.

To combat these issues, President Nixon consulted Federal Reserve Chairman Arthur Burns, incoming Treasury Secretary John Connally, and then undersecretary for international monetary affairs and future Federal Chairman Paul Volcker. On the afternoon of Friday, Aug. 13, 1971, these officials and other high-ranking White House and Treasury advisors met secretly with Nixon at Camp David. There was great debate about what Nixon should do, but ultimately Nixon, relying heavily on the advice of the self-confident Connally, decided to break up Bretton Woods by suspending the convertibility of the dollar into gold, freezing wages and prices for 90 days to combat potential inflationary effects, and impose an import surcharge of 10%. Connally brilliantly packaged the program not as America abandoning its commitment to the gold standard but as America taking charge. He turned, what would be the first American monetary default, which would have appeared shameful, into a moment of hubris.

> *"To prevent a run on the dollar, stabilize the US economy, and decrease US unemployment and inflation rates, on August 15, 1971, Nixon issued Executive Order 11615, pursuant to the Economic Stabilization Act of 1970, which imposed a 90-day maximum wage and price ceiling, a 10% import surcharge and most importantly, "closed the gold window", ending convertibility between U.S. dollars and gold."* (Wikipedia, 2014)

After Nixon's new policy went into effect, it seemed that all bets were off, and the grand global Ponzi scheme had begun. At which point the Federal Reserve could control anything it wanted in the federal money supply, allowing the banking cartels to the create fake interest rates, and exchange rates worldwide. This was one of the most fatal blows to economic stability in world history. Despite its drawbacks, the previous prevalence of gold as a failsafe ensured that the dollar could actually hold some form of accountability worldwide and that dollars could not just be printed willy-nilly, like they are today. Other than the removal of the Glass Stiegel Act in 1999, this was one of the most important events predicting the eventual demise of the dollar. These highly orchestrated evil economic decisions are why a global economic reset is inevitable, and how the beginnings of fiscal insanity came into being.

As previously noted, the final nail in the coffin of economic development was the repeal of the Glass Stiegel Act in 1999. It was none other than former President Bill Clinton, the other president who could not tell a lie, spearheaded this fine impediment to economic growth. The banks at the time lobbied and were able to remove these restrictions against total economic insanity, which gave rise to the age of the derivative, which is where we find ourselves at today.

This article from 2009 recounts how the repeal of this major protective piece of legislation ultimately lead to the mortgage crisis as well as the creation of another slew of financial instruments that were virtually worthless.

"Without the watering down and ultimate repeal of Glass-Steagall, the banks would have been barred from most of these activities," Demos said. "The market and appetite for derivatives would then have been far smaller, and Washington might not have felt a need to rescue the institutional victims."

But 10 years ago, the revocation of Glass-Steagall drew few critics. In the House; 155 Democrats and 207 Republicans voted for the measure, while 51 Democrats, 5 Republicans and 1 independent opposed it. Fifteen members did not vote. One of the leading voices of dissent was Senator Byron L. Dorgan, Democrat of North Dakota. He warned that reversing Glass-Stiegel and implementing the Republican-backed Gramm-Leach-Bliley Act was a mistake whose repercussions would be felt in the future.

"I think we will look back in 10 years' time and say we should not have done this, but we did because we forgot the lessons of the past, and that which is true in the 1930s is true in 2010," Mr. Dorgan said 10 years ago. "We have now decided in the name of modernization to forget the lessons of the past, of safety and of soundness."

Mr. Dorgan still feels the same way today. "I thought reversing Glass-Steagall would set us up for dramatic failure and that is exactly what has happened," the senator told DealBook on Thursday. "To fuse together the investment banking function with the F.D.I.C. banking function has proven to be a profound mistake." (Sanati, 2009)

As it stands now the dollar is still the biggest player worldwide, and even if countries want to get out of the dollar, there are not many places to run. The Eurozone crisis has ensured that the Euro is not the best option either for two important reasons. The first being that there are just not enough Euros in existence to replace dollars on a one-for-one basis. The second being the economic instability of Europe as a whole creates extensive liability for anyone holding mass quantities of the Euro.

The socialist policies of the European economic models has destroyed many once thriving merchant industrial economies, with no hope for policy shifts in site, Europe is stuck with a widening wealth gap as well. Further draconian regulation is all that has been seen for the past 10 years. These regulations will not do much to shore up the ailing

European economies. Germany has always been the workhorse of Europe, but Germany has quickly figured out what they signed on for is a hellish lesson in socialist welfare forcing them to bail out the rest of the ailing socialist economies of Europe.

> *"Increasingly, the German intelligentsia realizes the slippery slope it's on. But breaking out of the euro is always put aside in favor of being a team player and giving more financial assistance to the struggling south. Germany's ideology of a unified Europe reflects continued strong feelings of guilt from World War II. Unfortunately, it will be docile German workers who will pay the price, not the business and policy elite. Before the euro, German workers agreed to restrain their wages, receiving a rising currency and spending power in return. Now their restraint provides a surplus to fund the Mediterranean mess. Over the 11 years since the 2001 recession, Germany's real consumer spending is up a mere 6 percent, compared with 16 percent in France, 15 percent in Britain and 23 percent in the United States." (Duman, 2014)*

Commodity expert John Butler had this to say about the policies surrounding the hubris of the current economic leadership.

"Cash itself, of course, is at constant risk of devaluation, regardless of currency of denomination. Policymakers have made it abundantly clear that the value of cash is a policy tool, perhaps the single most important one there is. I regard it as highly unlikely that this thinking will change absent a future financial crisis that not only results in the death of the neo-Keynesian economic paradigm but also one that shows the current economic policy elite the door."

Trying to fix the dollar at this point is akin to putting humpty dumpty back together again. When an egg breaks into a million pieces, can it really be reassembled perfectly again? Even a team of Faberge egg masters would have a hard time putting this economic egg back together again. Although the United States currently enjoys the best financing interest rates worldwide, the honeymoon is about to be over. When the market correction comes, the leveling out of all these shenanigans will be fierce and it will take no prisoners.

It seems that as always, preparation is the key to prosperity, and the powers that be have prepared for a bubble of massive proportions. Although the United States has definitely become one of the most powerful nations as a result of having an Army backed Federal Reserve syndicate, the exporting of non-precious metal backed dollars is akin to selling the world hot air, and as history shows us, no economy is ever too big to fail. Just ask the ancient Romans, they will tell you all about it, tyrants caused their economies to fail time and time again, much to the dismay of the average Roman merchant.

3 The Petro Dollar

During the early 1970's the world witnessed the beginnings of the US Petro Dollar dominance. Oil backed dollar based transactions soon started to infiltrate the entire world, until the point we reached today, in which the dollar is synonymous with oil trade worldwide.

"Fully 85% of foreign-exchange transactions world-wide are trades of other currencies for dollars. What's more, what is true of foreign-exchange transactions is true of other international business. The Organization of Petroleum Exporting Countries sets the price of oil in dollars. The dollar is the currency of

denomination of half of all international debt securities. More

than 60% of the foreign reserves of central banks and

governments are in dollars. The greenback, in other words, is

not just America's currency. It's the worlds." (Eichengreen, 2014)

Let's start at the beginning. What is the petro dollar? Simply stated, the petro dollar is terminology that originated from the fact that during the 1900s, oil became a much more important natural resource than gold. Before the need for oil arose due to the industrial revolution, gold had been the king of the economic hill so to speak. Although the term itself wasn't coined until 1973, the petrodollar hegemony had been in place well before that, it was actually established on the heels of World War 2 and has been in place ever since.

"In the midst of World War II, Saudi Arabia secured a position of

enormous significance to the rising world power, America. With

its oil reserves essentially untapped, the House of Saud became

a strategic ally of immense importance, "a matter of national

security, nourishing U.S. military might and enhancing the

potentiality of postwar American hegemony." Saudi Arabia

welcomed the American interest as it sought to distance itself from its former imperial master, Britain, which it viewed with suspicion as the British established Hashemite kingdoms in the Middle East – the old rivals of the Saudis – in Jordan and Iraq.

The Saudi monarch, Abdul Aziz bin Abdul Rahman al Saud had to contend not only with the reality of Arab nationalism spreading across the Arab world (something which he would have to rhetorically support to legitimate his rule, but strategically maneuver through in order to maintain his rule), but he would also play off the United States and Great Britain against one another to try to ensure a better deal for 'the Kingdom', and ensure that his rivals – the Hashemites – in Jordan and Iraq did not spread their influence across the region. Amir (King) Abdullah of Transjordan – the primary rival to the Saudi king – sought to establish a "Greater Syria" following World War II, which would include Transjordan, Syria, Iraq, Lebanon and Palestine, and not to mention, the Hejaz province in Saudi Arabia." - Andrew Gavin (Gavin, 2014)

As this excerpt beautifully states, this partnership established large-scale political bargaining linking the United States and Saudi

Arabia. As the Saudis' are one of the top oil exporters in the world, they took it upon themselves to issue a dictatorial mandate, in which all transactions taking place involving Saudi oil would have to take place using the American dollar. Hence the Petro dollar was born.

"The number one American export is US dollars, more precisely the repayment of current dollars and promise of future dollars on loans to be received and goods to be imported by the USA. Like any fiat money it is paper currency backed up by absolutely nothing, but the rest of the world's need to import oil (for around 160 countries out of 200) means they need dollars to buy oil – when and if it is billed and settled in dollars. Other trade goods and services, in majority, are billed and settled in dollars, but there's no basic reason this has to be treated as permanent and obligatory. The same applies to oil.

As previously stated, the petrodollar system is above all political and concerns the US and Saudi Arabia before anybody else, or anything else. Due to current-ruling Saudi potentates, notably the so-called "Intelligence chief" Prince Bandar bin Sultan claiming Saudi rule over President Obama's decisions on Syrian bombing, and raging about Obama's non-bombing, the threat of

Saudi Arabia "abandoning the petrodollar" has been circulating.

When or if Saudi oil exports were increasingly billed and settled

in currencies other than the USD, the present semi-monopoly

would disintegrate." (Mckillop, 2014)

With the petro dollar system in place, any major world player with an appetite for oil would need to first purchase some U.S. dollars, with which to complete their billion dollar transactions. Although we could have made this a free market decision, allowing countries to willingly trade with us based on free market principles and the security of our currency, instead we chose to maintain a monopoly militarily. Anyone wanting to mess with Saudi Arabia, would first have to go through the United States oil contingent, and hence, the whole US military.

Politicians and military tacticians alike would be in an absolute uproar if this event took place because it would majorly effect their tactical operations, and the whole world power structure would be subject to review. Oil is very necessary to conduct warfare in the modern age. Without it, a country is unable to operate its, tanks, ships, or planes, and leaves them dependent upon the pre-world war two system of combat. Also known as fighting with swords, horses, and sailboats. As a quick historical anecdote, we can see how this strategy worked out for Poland during World War 2.

"The Polish army was able to mobilize one million men but was hopelessly outmatched in every respect. Rather than take a strong defensive position, troops were rushed to the front to confront the Germans and were systematically captured or annihilated. In a famously ill fated strategy, Polish commanders even sent horsed cavalry into battle against the heavy German armor. By September 8, German forces had reached the outskirts of Warsaw, having advanced 140 miles in the first week of the invasion.

The Polish armed forces hoped to hold out long enough so that an offensive could be mounted against Germany in the west, but on September 17 Soviet forces invaded from the east and all hope was lost."

Obviously it's only a matter of time before some superpower starts using alternative energy of one kind or another to power their tools of war, but as of now this hasn't been revealed publicly, and so oil is thought of as a major military objective to control. (It is rumored that Iran has been slowly converting to a form of plasma reactors, and possibly zero point energy, hence the elite were threatening to attack them, but who knows for sure.) Cutting off supply lines has always been a major military tactic, and probably one of the reasons that the United States has stockpiled so much oil overall. Just in case we are attacked and unable to produce our own oil for a stint of time, or if our supply from the Saudis is somehow cut off we could still have the Strategic Petroleum Reserve as a backup...

"The Strategic Petroleum Reserve (SPR) is an emergency fuel storage of oil maintained by the United States Department of Energy. It is the largest emergency supply in the world with the capacity to hold up to 727 million barrels (115,600,000 m3).

The current inventory is displayed on the SPR's website. As of December 21, 2012, the inventory was 694.9 million barrels (110,480,000 m3). This equates to 36 days of oil at current daily US consumption levels of 19.5 million barrels per day (3,100,000 m3/d). At recent market prices ($102 a barrel as of February

2012) the SPR holds over $26.7 billion in sweet crude and approximately $37.7 billion in sour crude (assuming a $15/barrel discount for sulfur content). The total value of the crude in the SPR is approximately $64.5 billion. The price paid for the oil is $20.1 billion (an average of $28.42 per barrel). Purchases of crude oil resumed in January 2009 using revenues available from the 2005 Hurricane Katrina emergency sale. The DOE purchased 10,700,000 barrels (1,700,000 m3) at a cost of $553 million. [4]

The United States started the petroleum reserve in 1975 after oil supplies were cut off during the 1973-74 oil embargo, to mitigate future temporary supply disruptions. According to the World Fact book, the United States imports a net 12 million barrels (1,900,000 m3) of oil a day (MMbd), so the SPR holds about a 58-day supply. However, the maximum total withdrawal capability from the SPR is only 4.4 million barrels (700,000 m3) per day, so it would take over 160 days to utilize the entire inventory." (Wikipedia, 2014)

So where is all of this heading? As we can see from past world conflicts; if we do decide to get into a major war again, it will undoubtedly be propped up by inordinate levels of hype, and lots of chest pounding on all sides. As it stands now the Saudis are upset that there plans to take over Iran, and other nations in the Middle East is going slower than planned. As well as the fact that the US has seemingly abandoned plans for an overt Israeli US Iran bombing which has failed due to a lack of public political support from the US public, and its military allies. Michael Snyder wrote a very interesting article tying all of these points together.

> *"Saudi Arabia desperately wants the U.S. military to intervene in the Syrian civil war on the side of the "rebels". This has not happened yet, and the Saudis are very upset about that. Of course the Saudis could always go and fight their own war, but that is not the way that the Saudis do things."*

So since the Saudis are not getting their way, they are threatening to punish the U.S. for their inaction. According to Reuters, the Saudis are saying that "all options are on the table now"..."

Snyder goes on to say that:

> *"In 2012, the United States ran a trade deficit of about $540,000,000,000 with the rest of the planet. In other words,*

about half a trillion more dollars left the country than came into

the country. These dollars represent the number one "product"

that the U.S. exports. We make dollars and exchange them for

the things that we need. Major exporting countries (such as

Saudi Arabia) take many of those dollars and "invest" them in

our debt at ultra-low interest rates. It is this system that makes

our massively inflated standard of living possible.

When this system ends, the era of cheap imports and super low

interest rates will be over and the "adjustment" to our standard

of living will be excruciatingly painful. And without a doubt, the

day is rapidly approaching when the petrodollar monopoly will

end. Today, Russia is the number one exporter of oil in the

world.

China is now the number one importer of oil in the world, and at

this point they are actually importing more oil from Saudi Arabia

than the United States is." (Snyder, 2014)

Although the collapse of the petrodollar won't exclusively

eliminate the dollar as the world reserve currency, and cause a Global

Economic Reset within itself, it is definitely a lynchpin in a serious game of economic Jenga happening worldwide. It seems that the people in charge of the global banking system just love to gamble with other people's lives, because this is one hell of a game of economic Russian roulette that is going on. If we lose just a few more trading partners, the whole house of cards can come tumbling down. Sadly the United States used to export ideas, aka patents on electricity, cars, electronics, and other inventions, now our main exports are fear, fiat currency, warfare, oil, and bull crap in the form of gross political rhetoric.

There are many different economic theories on how the collapse of the petrodollar will play out, and none of them seem particularly peachy for the good old stars and stripes. One such scenario is as follows:

"Right now, the US Dollar makes up 2/3rds of the world's global reserve currency. This is because nearly every oil-exporting country in the world exclusively sells their oil in dollars, so nations are forced to hoard large amounts of the dollar.

There are two countries that don't sell their oil in the dollar: Syria, and Iran.

If these two countries joined forces, got Venezuela on their side, maybe a few other countries, and then made an economic treaty with the BRICS nations, an acronym for Brazil, Russia, India, China, and South Africa, to buy their oil in a currency other than the US dollar, the economy would collapse.

All countries in the world would send their massive hoards of the dollar back to the Fed in exchange for whichever currency replaces it. The value of the dollar would shrink dramatically and the Fed would be forced to take steps to shrink the money supply to stem massive inflation. The raising of the Federal Funds rate would mean that there would not be enough new loans created to pay off old loans (which is necessary, because there is always more debt in the economy than there is money, because money is created with interest attached, from the very beginning we are all indebted to a small cabal that sits behind the federal reserve). The defaulting of loans would lead to a chain reaction that would collapse the $700,000,000,000,000 derivatives market. In addition, the Fed wouldn't be able to mindlessly pump money into the economy anymore such as with their current policy of quantitative easing." (Abbey, 2013)

Whichever scenario ends up playing out, the motto of the story should be, be prepared for anything; for a life lived in fear, is not worth living. Being preparing for the worst, and hoping for the best is never a bad plan. Whatever happens, we just can't let fear become our primary motive, for someone living in fear is a slave to himself or herself. If you can't control yourself, history shows us that someone will always take it upon himself or herself to try and control you instead. Self-sustainability, and the emergence of the United States as a superpower, happened because the nation was determined to succeed, and do it our own way. Although we may have had to reinvent the wheel here and there, overall the United States has done a pretty dang good job keeping itself together and allowing people enough freedom to make things happen in a semi-free market. Sure we may not all be born rich, smart, or attractive, but we all have the ability to overcome our inner limitations, and establish ourselves as good moral people who serve to bring harmony to a world in which existential pain is so pervasive. As I often voice to my listeners on my daily podcast, run as fast as you can from government dependence. Empower yourself and take on the mantle of maximum personal responsibility and self-reliance.

4 Cracks in the System

Throughout time, we can look at economic cycles and identify different repeating scenarios, in an attempt to make sense of the current economic circumstances, and predict future trends based upon past realities. Thereby giving us a bellwether in order to gauge the overall volatility level of our economic cycle. In our age, people seem to think that hard times will never fall upon the strong and mighty United States of America. Yes, many people believe that America is some kind of unshakable eagle atop the golden pillars of Liberty. Unfortunately this is far from the truth. One only has to watch Team America a few times to realize that America lost the moral high ground long ago, and without morality, you don't have much. Morally speaking, America is a very questionable place because of the globalist policies that have been instituted; and America is just as liable as any other country to fall victim to its own machinations.

It is a sad fact that the social engineers always see the need to take things just a bit too far in order to push the limits of human experience to new highs, or new lows. Although in some senses you could say that we have taken the world economic system hostage via force and petro dollars, this is ultimately a very unstable economic reality. Fiat money is merely a concept built upon trust, convenience, and the threat of force. Without the threat of force, trust, or inherent value within the currency (i.e. precious metals), fiat money becomes worthless, as we will learn in later chapters. To give us some perspective on the worst case scenario regarding a governments miss management of a currency, we can again look to historical examples. One would figure that the worst hyperinflation ever seen would have been hundreds of years ago, right? Wrong, try Yugoslavia in 1993, where the currency was devalued to 1 quadrillionth (that's right you heard it correctly) of its former value. Under the leadership of a bunch of economic buffoons, with extreme micromanagement leanings, the following scenario occurred.

> *"By the early 1990s the government used up all of its own hard currency reserves and proceeded to loot the hard currency savings of private citizens. It did this by imposing more and more difficult restrictions on private citizens' access to their hard currency savings in government banks.*

The government operated a network of stores at which goods were supposed to be available at artificially low prices. In practice these stores seldom had anything to sell and goods were only available at free markets where the prices were far above the official prices that goods were supposed to sell at in government stores. In particular, all of the government gasoline stations eventually were closed and gasoline was available only from roadside dealers whose operation consisted of a parked car with a plastic can of gasoline sitting on the hood. The market price was the equivalent of $8 per gallon." (Watkins, 2014)

Sadly, it doesn't end there....

"The government tried to counter the inflation by imposing price controls. But when inflation continued the government price controls meant the price producers were getting ridiculous low and they stopped producing. In October of 1993 the bakers stopped making bread and Belgrade was without bread for a week. The slaughter houses refused to sell meat to the state stores and this meant meat became unavailable for many sectors of the population. Other stores closed down holding their

inventory rather than sell their goods at the government mandated prices. When farmers refused to sell to the government at the artificially low prices the government dictated, government irrationally used hard currency to buy food from foreign sources rather than remove the price controls. The Ministry of Agriculture also risked creating a famine by selling farmers only 30 percent of the fuel they needed for planting and harvesting.

"Later the government tried to curb inflation by requiring stores to file paperwork every time they raised a price. This meant that many of the stores employees had to devote their time to filling out these government forms. Instead of curbing inflation this policy actually increased inflation because the stores tended to increase prices by a bigger jump so that they would not have to file forms for another price increase so soon." (Watkins, 2014)

The bankruptcy of the United States can be seen in multitudes of different ways, many of which are complex and convoluted, but overall nothing about our books is balanced, and the big banks have infected every area of the government balance sheets, so there's no easy way out. To perpetuate the Ponzi scheme the United States keeps three different sets of books at any given time. This allows for investors to be hoodwinked into believing the United States runs some sort of a tight fiscal ship when it does anything but. It is common for corporations to maintain two sets of books when they reach a certain size, as it offers multitudes of different tax incentives to the modern mega corporation. This practice is also very common amongst the public and private college Universities nationwide who commonly use two sets of books to horde their billions in offshore endowment money from donors, while simultaneously raising tuition prices. (Nice guys right?)

"In the world of tax legislation, hedge funds are the hot topic. The same could be said for the world of university endowment portfolios. Both were scrutinized in a hearing on Wednesday as the Senate Committee on Finance set its sights on the insurance and reinsurance industries, offshore tax havens and, of course, the high-yield but potentially volatile financial products.

Hedge funds have been controversial, in part, because of the low tax rates reserved for their managers, but they've netted some impressive gains -- as well as recent losses -- for investors, prominent among them university endowments. Stagnating state and federal support for higher education and the ever-increasing price tag have only intensified calls for closer scrutiny of endowments, and specifically, questions about why universities don't withdraw more from their holdings to boost their financial aid offerings or even, in some cases, cover tuition entirely." (Guess, 2007)

For the sake of the brevity, we will look at the top five reasons why the United States is on the verge of a monumental economic shift.

Derivatives

What is a Derivative? According to Investopia.com it consists of the following:

"A derivative is a contract between two or more parties whose value is based on an agreed-upon underlying financial asset, index or security. Common underlying instruments include: bonds, commodities, currencies, interest rates, market indexes and stocks. Futures contracts, forward contracts, options, swaps and warrants are common derivatives. A futures contract, for example, is a derivative because its value is affected by the

performance of the underlying contract. Similarly, a stock option is a derivative because its value is "derived" from that of the underlying stock.

Derivatives are used for speculating and hedging purposes. Speculators seek to profit from changing prices in the underlying asset, index or security. For example, a trader may attempt to profit from an anticipated drop in an index's price by selling (or going "short") the related futures contract. Derivatives used as a hedge allow the risks associated with the underlying asset's price to be transferred between the parties involved in the contract." (Investopia, 2014)

Put into plain English, derivatives are a form of banking "asset" that was concocted to confuse people by bundling different types of assets together, in order to make sure nobody could ever know what the true value of the asset was. Hence, the brokers can claim the fake paper asset is worth more than it is, and charge accordingly. Another analogy would be like using big words around small children in order to confuse them into not caring about what you're talking about. Even if what you're saying directly pertains to them, they won't be able to catch your drift. Just to be clear; derivatives are the smoking gun, the elephant in the room, the unclothed emperor all rolled into one.

They are the source of 80-90% of the depravity going on within the financial markets, and the global economy in general. Until they are dealt with once and for all nothing will change for the better fiscally speaking. Sure any Joe off the street could become a profiteer by buying and selling these things if you are educated in these fiscal reindeer games. Yet long term no one can retain anything of value within a system based upon unsound fiscal principals where the big banks are leveraged 70 to 1 and one false move could bring down the entire financial system. Creating fake money out of thin air and selling it to others is still thievery no matter how you try to spin it otherwise.

To simplify things let's take a look at the game Monopoly. Remember that when you used to play as a little kid, sometimes the person who was the banker would end up with an extra couple five hundred dollar bills at the end? Multiply that times about a trillion, and that is how far astray our economic balance sheets have gone. It seems as though the big megabanks in collusion with the federal reserve have issued enough digital money and sold enough derivative based assets, to where nobody really knows what the difference between a common hedge fund bond and a piece of toilet paper. The really insane part is that the criminals don't even know what these fake derivatives are worth anymore either. The best way I can describe it, is a children's game of telephone gone incredibly wrong. The assets have been sold so many times that it's hard to know what is what anymore. They have stolen so much, and created so many fake assets that even the bankers with their armies of accountants, and fake tax preparers can't calculate how much toxic derivative debt really exists out in the global markets let alone what the global implications worldwide might be when all of this goes bust.

If you wanted to equate the state of the economy to illness, you could equate it to a stage-four cancer patient. The patient may survive, but they may lose a limb or two in the process. Sometimes it's best to just start over and admit the model is unsustainable long-term. It's not just the American people who have been conned by this system either. It's a global phenomenon waiting to go bust in a country near you. The best-case scenario of the derivative bubble looks like what happened in Iceland. The country was declared bankrupt for a few weeks, the people protested, kicked the criminal bankers out, and life was back to normal within a few months. (See Chapter 7 for a full breakdown.)

Derivatives have long been sought after by the global banking elite in order to manufacture their engineered control grid. Although the British had monetary control mechanisms in place during the last century in a half, the overall global trade network had not yet become sophisticated enough to pull off a global Ponzi scheme of this magnitude.

Unfunded Mandates

Unfunded mandates include any government expenditures, which have been mandated by the congress to be paid for, but for which there is no active revenue source with which to generate such an income stream to pay for. The biggest unfunded liabilities are social security, Medicare and Medicaid. According to Harvard historian and economist Niall Ferguson:

> *"The most recent estimate for the difference between the net present value of federal government liabilities and the net present value of future federal revenues is over $200 trillion, nearly thirteen times the debt as stated by the U.S. Treasury."*

Unfunded mandates can range from pensions plans with scheduled 5% pay increases, to bridges scheduled to be built in 2030. Long story short, the government's mouth is writing checks that their ass can't cash. One of the leading authorities on this subject is the previous comptroller general for the United States, David M. Walker. Mr. Walker runs a website entitled *deficitranger.com*, in which he regularly attempts to dissuade politicians from spending indiscriminately and breaks down the after effects of what will happen if we do keep on this trajectory:

"The term "fiscal exposures" measures a range of federal liabilities, programs and activities which, based on current law, will require federal resources at a future date. A complete accounting of the current major fiscal exposures provides a fuller and fairer picture of the deteriorating condition of federal finances. As the preceding table shows, the federal government was in a $56 trillion-plus hole as of September 30, 2008 and the hole gets deeper by $2-3 trillion per year, even with a balanced federal budget."

Some exposures are explicit and known liabilities that the federal government is legally obligated to fulfill. Commitments and contingencies represent contractual requirements that the federal government is expected to fulfill when or if specified conditions are met.

The largest category of exposure contains the growing unfunded promises for Social Security and Medicare benefits for current and future beneficiaries. Although people rely on the promise of those benefits, the Congress and the President can— and at times do—change the programs in ways that increase or decrease the value of expected benefits, and thus alter the size of the implicit exposure. For example, in the past, policymakers have increased payroll tax contributions, increased the retirement eligibility age, changed cost-of-living adjustments, and increased beneficiary premiums applicable to such programs. In addition, the U.S. Supreme Court has ruled that the benefits under these programs can be changed at any time through legislation.

Following the downgrade of the US debt rating from its coveted triple A status in 2011, markets have begun the slow road home, in an attempt to ditch the dollar--desperately hoarding assets, and trying to find safe places to store wealth within their home nations. The dollar presents a conundrum for the entire world, as there are not many places to run for shelter.

"First of all, the U.S. downgrade will force a reassessment of the entire concept of risk in the global economy. The U.S. has been considered the world's safest investment, the standard by which all other economies are judged. But if the U.S. isn't as safe as it once was, a domino effect may be felt throughout the world. If the U.S. doesn't warrant a triple-A, we have to ask: Which country does? France, for example, is rated AAA, but it has a similar level of government debt as the U.S. (each around 94% of GDP in 2010), and the economy doesn't have any better growth prospects. So if the U.S. doesn't deserve an AAA, does France? And if such stalwarts of the global economy are riskier than they were before, what does that mean for countries with lower ratings? Should they be downgraded further?

In the short term, that thinking likely means greater uncertainty in global markets, especially in Europe. If the U.S. isn't triple-A, what does that tell us about Italy and Spain? The S&P

downgrade could well put even more pressure on Europe's weak

economies and on European leaders to act to stem the crisis."

(Schuman, 2014)

As it turns out, Obama was the fraud a minority of Americans knew he would be, a pawn of the banking cartels. He has done almost nothing to fix our economic woes. In fact, he has done the exact opposite. Contrary to the pitch sold to Americans, Obamacare solves none of the existing healthcare problems, rather it only serves to make our system much more complex. Obamacare is doubling and tripling most people's health care costs, and millions have been cancelled from their existing plans. The key is, spend less government money, and give tax dollars back to people so they can take care of themselves. If you can stop the psychological co-dependence within our society, people will be forced to rely upon themselves, and as a result a much more natural way of life will emerge but if there's one thing we can be sure of, it's that the majority American politicians hate a strong community unit. For where there are small tight knit communities practicing self-sufficiency, the government is rendered useless. Who needs a government when you are totally self-sufficient, and living with a group of people that you enjoy? The lesson is simple--a smaller government means a happier freer people. The less self-sufficient you are, the more the government will be able to tell you what to do. When the government tells you what to do, and what you can have, are you really free? Governments such as this rob your hard earned money, just to become your master. So it's really no surprise that we have ended up with a system that has hundreds of trillions in unfunded mandates. Unfunded mandates are the checks that the government is writing to itself, so it can continue to be your pimp and skim off the top of everything you do. It's the monkey on our back, and the bogeyman in our closet. I think Morpheus says it best in the Matrix:

"Do you want to know what it is? The matrix is everywhere; it's all around us, even now in this very room. You can see it when you look out your window or when you turn on your TV. You can feel it when you go to work, when you go to church, when you pay your taxes. It is the world that has been pulled over your eyes to blind you from the truth. What truth? That you are a slave Neo, like everyone else, you were born into bondage, born into a prison that you cannot smell or taste or touch. A prison for your mind. Unfortunately, no one can be told what the

Matrix is. You have to see what it is for yourself." – (The Matrix, 1999)

Unfunded mandates are one of the prime reasons why a global economic reset would be a good thing. It would totally wipe out the vast majority of debt, and give our grandchildren a clean slate from which to work from. They would no longer be cursed, by the idiotic political ramblings of the flower children and baby boomers.

Corporate Welfare and Tax Loopholes

Mega multi-national corporations within the United States routinely pay almost nothing in taxes. Granted this is only the top 1% of the mega corporations, those who are able to lobby congress to open up these international loopholes. Generally speaking these complex tax-shielding structures involve funneling the money through 2-3 different countries in an attempt to claim the income is not taxable via US law. This style of tax avoidance is a pretty complex process, but nothing is that difficult if you have a small army of accountants to rig it all up for you. This Reuters article recounts the recent history of just such practices...

"Thirty large and profitable U.S. corporations paid no income taxes in 2008 through 2010, said a study on Thursday that arrives as Congress faces rising demands for tax reform but seems unable or unwilling to act. Pepco Holdings Inc., a Washington, D.C.-area Power Company, had the lowest effective tax rate, at negative 57.6 percent, among the 280 Fortune 500 companies studied. The statutory U.S. corporate income tax rate is 35 percent, one of the highest in the world; but over the 2008-2010 period, very few of the companies studied paid it, said the report. The average effective tax rate for the companies over the period was 18.5 percent, said Citizens for Tax Justice and the Institute on Taxation and Economic Policy, both think tanks."

Their report also listed General Electric Co, Paccar Inc., PG&E Corp, Computer Sciences Corp, Boeing Co and NiSource Inc. as among the 30 that paid no taxes. It was also recently revealed that tech giant Apple was paying around 1% in corporate taxes. Now that's Apple were talking about here, not the dollar store.

"Apple used technicalities in Irish and American tax law to pay little or no corporate taxes on at least $74 billion over the past four years, according to the Senate panel's findings. The investigation found no evidence that Apple did anything illegal. Aides to the subcommittee said they have never seen a company use a subsidiary that didn't owe corporate income taxes to any country." (Wall Street Journal, 2014)

If we can't figure out that there's something wrong with one of the biggest household names in the entire world not paying any income tax, then we need to have a serious debate about overall public policy. The 1% of 1% is getting richer and the middle class is shrinking, stuck eking out a living and being taxed at around 50%. I mean it's no wonder that these companies don't want to pay income taxes, who would? The real problem is that the worker pays everything while the company pays nothing. Good old Ross Perot could have fixed a lot of this in the mid 90's. He had the genius plan of shutting down the good old IRS and going to a flat tax on all goods sold. Making sure the government gets their cut, while cutting out the middleman worldwide. Of course this would make way too much sense to ever be implemented by the criminal politicians in Washington.

One of the top Rothschild bankers Georges C. Karlwe, is himself admitted to the magnitude of this crisis in an open letter stating the following:

"For 30 months now central banks have been injecting hundreds of billions of dollars, Euros and what have you into the global economy. For centuries, ever since currencies were invented, Caesars, sovereigns, dictators and democracies have been reducing the quantity of gold in coins and replacing it with cheaper metals. More recently they have simply added zero's to banknotes or to book entries. Never to this day have central banks been able to withdraw the "capital" — so much hot air — that they have pumped into the mains nearly free of interest. On the face of it this time will be no different."

He also went on to say in his final analysis that he felt this was the most probable outcome of such efforts:

"We are probably witnessing the last years of our civilization — or what remains of it."

The Internet is the sole reason that such a global currency price fixing was possible. Going back to the history of the Internet's creation, we quickly realize that this too was concocted with spurious government plans in mind. Every day, thousands of traders who are specially placed by the mega banks make vast trades to stabilize markets that naturally would run towards a correction. In real terms this would mean that if markets were truly "free", we would be seeing vastly higher interest rates, and gold valued at double or triple what it stands at today. Sadly it seems that everyone and their mother bought into this derivatives lie, and was willing to dole out hundreds of thousands in public and privately funded investments. All of this was done to support the addiction of the schemers on Wall Street. Upon further investigation you will realize that everything from bridges, to railroads, to pension funds, to grandma's 401k, all ended up within the confines of the derivative junk market. Now all of the real assets are losing their worth because they have been tied to the deadweight junk paper assets. They are literally throwing good money after bad so to speak.

Instigation of this kind of manipulation wouldn't seem so insane, until you start to realize that the people who created the mess in the first place have no long term solutions and profit from the crisis. The system as is stands is meant to fail, only to further consolidate power of the global financial planners. It's like a little kid who wanders into a museum and breaks all the timeless pieces of art, and then being asked to restore them back to their original state. The kid has just learned how to tie his shoes, how can you expect him to know how to recreate a masterpiece that took millions of man-hours to complete? Well, you can't. So we have the primary dilemma forcing such a global economic reset. No amount of economic super geniuses could ever figure out this Gordian knot. We will soon find out as a populace that the only way out is to cut off the problem at the source, as the mythical story of the Gordian knot shows us. This economic time bomb is set to blow, and we are going to be left high and dry by those forces that created it. If Houdini can't do it, how could Bernanke or Yellen? With all the kings' horses and all the kings' men, we can't put a derivatives based economy back together again. And what, might you ask do we receive as the global taxpayer funding this whole game of 3D algorithm stock market Russian roulette? Unless you're living it up in a penthouse near Wall Street or in a castle in Switzerland, and taking spiritual debauchery to new levels, then probably not much.

Generally speaking you can't find even a hint of consternation from the Bernie Madoffs, Jamie Dimons or the Lloyd Blakefeins of the world. Although if you look closely you will see some legitimate concern from time to time on the face of Janet Yellen and Ben Bernanke. Even though Bernanke is a proven liar and banker shill, he still subconsciously understands the magnitude of the implosion of this system, and the damage it will cause worldwide. Deep down Janet Yellen the current Federal Reserve chair seems to know how hellish this Global Economic Reset will be when it all flushes out. She tells everyone that the bubbles won't burst, that prices on everything will stabilize, and that this is no cause for concern. Sadly this is not the case, and probably won't be for the next 10-15 years until after this whole reset scenario has happened. Everyone knows that even the most ruthless sociopath can only believe their own lies for so long, before the truth comes in like a cold shower to snap people back into reality. Whether that shower of truth comes in the form of a personal tragedy, or a public humiliation is yet to be seen.

As we all know, karma is hellish, and this is why it's important to work on helping people within the system to extricate themselves from the treachery, and to help reform the system by first reforming themselves. We need not view the politicians as our enemies, as it is much more constructive to view them as examples of how not to live. As long as humanity runs in the exact opposite direction of these gremlins we will be in good shape.

To create an economic bubble in the name of profiteering is one thing; obviously that's an egregious offense within itself. However to perpetuate the bubble in the name of a controlled collapse is quite another. Anyone who has ever planned a big event such as a wedding or a banquet, knows how much of a pain in the keister it can be. It can take months and months of planning for an event that lasts for just 5-6 hours. In many cases, by the time the event actually arrives, you're already ready for it to be over. (Ask many brides after their weddings and they will tell you that they would rather have had the 10-50k in the bank rather than the whole dog and pony show.) This is the phase where I think the global financial planners are psychologically; they have wanted this for so long that they almost don't want it anymore. The brass tacks of the situation are that there is no good way to orchestrate a collapse of this magnitude gracefully. In the words of Walter from the motion picture the Big Lebowski "When a plan gets too complex, too many things can go wrong."

Eventually, people will reap what they sow within the financial markets, and no amount of money can shield someone from the existential hell they have created living toxic lives, and destroying the lives of others. Nor can money prevent you from good old-fashioned bad luck. Fortunately, the good and moral people of the world will always be willing to help pick up the pieces, and restore sanity. Human nature is not all bad, and societies do end up craving a bit of sanity from time to time—especially after these kinds of scenarios play out...which is well documented historically. When you witness firsthand just how hellish human behavior can be, who wouldn't want to go back towards a system of peace and prosperity?

Capital Controls and Currency Restrictions

Capital controls and currency restrictions are one of the biggest precursors towards a global economic reset. Globally, currency restrictions have always triggered panic within the markets, and are designed to do just that. When you can't access your own money, there is always a reason to be concerned, and people are not that stupid. Most recently HSBC has been preventing its clients from large cash withdrawals without proof of a "prior need".

"If you bank at HSBC in England, don't plan on making any large cash withdrawals. At least not without a good explanation. Or, maybe even a permission slip. That's because a previously unannounced change in banking policy is blocking some customers from making large

withdrawals without "evidence" explaining why they need the money from their accounts. The policy affects customers attempting withdrawals for amounts as little as £5,000 ($8,253).

HSBC says it's all done in the name of customer protection.

"We have an obligation to protect our customers, and to minimize the opportunity for financial crime," HSBC said in a statement. "However, following feedback, we are immediately updating guidance to our customer facing staff to reiterate that it is not mandatory for customers to provide documentary evidence for large cash withdrawals, and on its own, failure to show evidence is not a reason to refuse a withdrawal. We are writing to apologize to any customer who has been given incorrect information and inconvenienced."

Closer to home, Chase has also decided to start imposing currency restrictions by limiting the amount of cash withdrawals that customers can take out daily, as well as out and out banning international wire transfers on many accounts. If this does not sound like the beginning of a Soviet Eastern bloc-style economy, I don't know what is. The banksters are not stupid; they know that in the beginning of any collapse, people with large amounts of cash reserves will try their best to get their money out of the country. The currency controls allow them to head this scenario off at the pass, by cutting citizens off at the source. Mainstream media has been dead silent on this subject, which is no big surprise as they are also on the banker payroll. Eventually the other media outlets were briefly forced to address it. But even today if you search this in Google, it's a virtual black hole, you can't find anything, very ominous indeed.

"I personally visited Chase Bank and inquired about setting up an account and asked if I could wire money out of the country or withdraw the amounts of cash listed in their letter. I was told no, and that I would have to "qualify" with them for a special type of international bank account and would have to deposit huge amounts of money and pay fees to be able to access those services.

What this constitutes is a war on cash and a war on small business and individuals. Two years ago we saw a giant backlash against Bank of America when they announced customers would be charged for using their own money via their debit card. We have crossed the Rubicon where now the currency has been so devalued that you will have to pay fees to have your money in a bank or use a debit card.

In saying that international wire transfers are too much of a risk, Chase Bank might as well be bankrupt because it is telling you there is no money to withdraw." (Watson, 2014)

Historically speaking, currency restrictions always precipitate a collapse. It has happened umpteen times, and might happen again right here in the U.S. of A. So this is one of the biggest red flags, and means that they are going to beta test a collapse by imposing just such restrictions. This way they can see how much public backlash there is for their actions, as well as just how far they can push the sheeple, before they push back.

State and Local Government Bankruptcies

The Federal Government isn't the only one having a problem balancing the books. Many local level governments are also having a hard time keeping the ship afloat. After Detroit filed for bankruptcy in 2013 it has come out that other cities are also on the brink of fiscal collapse, as detailed below. Detroit's bankruptcy filing sent shivers down the spine of municipal bondholders, government employees, and big-city urban residents all over the country. That's because many of the 61 largest U.S. cities are plagued with the same kinds of retirement legacy costs that sent Detroit into Chapter 9 bankruptcy in the summer of 2013.

These cities have amassed $118 billion in unfunded healthcare liabilities. These are legal promises to pay healthcare benefits to municipal workers beyond the employee contributions to finance those funds. This is a giant fiscal sinkhole and because of defined benefit plans, the hole keeps getting deeper. While Detroit may be the largest city in American history to go bankrupt, but it is not alone. The city raced to the financial insolvency finish line before anyone else in its class. Keep an eye on "too big to fail" cities like Chicago, Philadelphia and New York.

"According to an analysis by the Manhattan Institute, several Chicago pension funds are in worse financial shape than the worker pensions in Detroit. One is only 25 percent funded, and where the other 75 percent of the money will come from is anyone's guess. And there are about a dozen major California

cities having systemic problems paying their bills." –Steven

Moore

Who ends up paying for all of these bankruptcies you ask? Of course as always, it's the federal government, along with local taxpayers, yet who answers the questions about what happens when the feds go bankrupt? Who bails them out? One of the most difficult parts of maintaining a city in today's day and age are is the rising cost of pension plans. Most city pension plans have automatic pay raises built in every year.

So let's say you're a city lifeguard. No matter what you do, as long as you don't get fired, you will most likely get a 3-5% pay raise yearly. So say you work 30 years for the city and start out at $15 an hour. That puts your pay up to around $30-$37 dollars by the time you retire. Now if you get full retirement on top of that the city will pay you around 60-80% of your full working wage for the rest of your life. So if you retire at 65, the city might have to pay that for 25 to 35 years depending on how long you live. The city will in effect be paying you $30 an hour to do nothing, even though you were a minimally skilled worker to begin with. I'm not trying to bash lifeguards; I'm just trying to point out that this scenario would never happen in the private sector.

Had the cities been extremely astute in managing the investment fund assets, the pension funds might not be such a big issue. The problem has become the fact that all of these city pension funds ended up getting mixed in with the derivatives. Which in turn makes the pension funds virtually worthless in many cases. Being that derivatives are good candidates for being the least sound financial investment humanity has ever created. Many of the cities that aren't suffering from derivative problems are instead contesting shortfalls in tax revenue, due to drops in local corporate profitability and the collapse of housing prices in 2008. When the corporations are taking loses, so are the cities. As you can imagine, this ends up starting a massive domino effect. The cities then respond by hiking up taxes on the businesses in town that have remained profitable. This policy effectively drives the profitable businesses out of town, out of state, or overseas depending. Cities don't seem to understand that higher taxes mean less profits for the corporations, and the people employed by them. Bureaucrats never seem to see the long-term consequences of their actions, but hey as long as the government survives, to hell with everything else right?

5 The World Begins to Ditch the Dollar

As popular as the dollar may seem in 2014, a mass exodus from dollars is definitely possible and trends have begun to emerge to that effect. Although the cost for foreign countries to switch their currency reserves away from dollars and into other currencies is prohibitive—it's still a better option than a total loss of value, which is possible. Countries are willing to go to great lengths to preserve their fiscal prosperity, and rightfully so. Many of them are aware they are dealing with the devil, but are having a difficult time extricating themselves from the system as it stands today. On the surface, it looks like the Federal Reserve really wants the global economy to go bust—and they do, to an extent. But long term, if they cut off all money, they also cut off the source of their own power, so it's hard to say they want to crash things worldwide. A piece by piece approach is much more likely. This way they can come in to pick up the pieces while living cozy precocious lives in their underground bunkers or in their offshore island estates. This dystopia dream of mass bankruptcy within America has happened before during the great depression. Which was yet another banker engineered collapse.

"Thus, it was one of those backstairs, backdoor meetings, which aimed in a way at the destruction of the Federal Reserve Board itself. When you desire to stabilize the value of gold, you have to cooperate with other countries, and mostly with their central banks. The secret meetings between the Federal Reserve Board Governors and heads of the European central banks were not held to stabilize anything, but rather to talk about the best way of getting the gold held in the United States by the Federal Reserve System back to Europe—and also to get the nations of that continent back on the gold standard."

"The League of Nations had not yet succeeded in doing that because the U.S. Senate had refused to let Woodrow Wilson betray us to an international monetary authority. It took the Second World War and FDR to do that. In fact, Europe needed the gold, which we had, and the Federal Reserve System stealthily gave it to them, $500 million worth. The passage of that gold out of the U.S. caused the deflation of the stock boom and the collapse of business prosperity in the 1920s, resulting in the Great Depression. Mullins comments that it was the worst calamity which has ever befallen this nation." –Jerry Mazza

The great depression was another banker created crisis, and one that was not half as dangerous as the time bomb we face today. Yet the bottom line is that Americans are a resilient group of people, and with the advent of the Internet, people will be able to teach themselves the necessary adaptive crisis skills necessary for survival. (At least the children of the Internet generation will be able to.) A healthy dose of realism will bring a lot of value to the coddled populace. If we can be honest with ourselves, and honest with friends about the times that face us, then we can use this crisis as a means for positive change. Spiritually adaptable and morally grounded people will be able to quickly surmise the appropriate actions required to harmonize their lives within any economic environment.

One of the first major indicators of the flight out of dollars would be the price of gold, as we can look to gold as a benchmark of general global currency valuation. When gold rises, all the other paper currencies lose a little bit of real time purchasing power. Gold has already risen well over the $1,400 marking a three-fold increase in less than a decade. Surely someone other than the United States consumer, and the Chinese treasury is getting the message that inflation within the U.S. dollar might soon become a big issue. According to leading Austrian economists real time estimates indicate that true inflation is running somewhere between 8-10 percent a year, and growing.

"McDonald's has killed the dollar menu because it is becoming impossible to "make any money selling burgers for $1".

But don't worry – the government says that the inflation you see is just your imagination.

-Amazon.com has raised the minimum order size required for free shipping from $25 to $35."

We must in turn reference that this massive inflation (which isn't even keeping pace with the QE1, or QE2 trillion dollar cash infusions.)" (Info Wars, 2014)

Inflation on the ground level can be hard to see, but as we analyze the rising prices associated with staples such as milk, eggs, and bread, we see inflation happening on a base level. These basic everyday foods are always a great indicator of real time inflation. Prices for coffee, fruit, bacon, pasta and a slew of other food items have registered gains over the past year as high as 40%. In April 2014 alone, grapes went up nearly 30%, cabbage jumped about 17% and orange juice surged more than 5%.

"This is a serious problem in the middle- to lower-income parts of the country," says Richard Hastings, consumer strategist at Global Hunter Securities in Newport Beach, Calif. "A little bit of inflation in the United States is actually a big problem because of how many lower-income people we have. It's a serious long-term fiscal problem." -Jeff Cox CNBC

This inflation trend is just adding fuel to the fire, and exhibiting the even more dangerous long-term trend of fiscal insanity, and irresponsibility. If none of these problems are addressed, circumstances will have no choice but to get worse. Reality does not make exceptions for the insane. John Butler, a revered author on the topic of global reserve currency states:

"There are some things about which we can be relatively certain, however. If the dollar continues to gradually lose reserve currency status, or does so abruptly in a future financial crisis, it will reinforce the stag-flationary economic conditions already prevailing in the US and in many other countries. Import

prices will rise, yet growth will remain subdued given that the capital base is being consumed."

In another telling article he discloses the status of the current gold market conditions abroad. Venezuela is now joining the growing list of countries that want their gold back.

"Venezuela's decision to take delivery of its gold places additional focus on the unique role that physical gold plays in the global economy. In recent months, the central banks of Mexico, South Korea, Bangladesh and Kazakhstan have bought gold on the open market. Others no doubt continue to accumulate gold less overtly. Why? If there was growing faith in the dollar-centric global financial system, would central banks be accumulating gold reserves at the fastest pace since the 1970s?

No, on the contrary, this trend is a clear indication that global confidence in the dollar continues to erode. Should more countries line up to take physical delivery of their gold, rather than leave it in US custody, it would be a sign that confidence in the US itself, as a safe and reliable jurisdiction for global commerce, is also beginning to erode." (The Butterflies of

August, 2011)

China is obviously the beginning and end of most world reserve currency discussions, as they hold most of the reserve dollars and treasury notes. Hence they have the most to lose if the dollar goes belly up. China has been talking tough, and expressing their disgust for U.S. fiscal policy for almost a decade now. Obviously the U.S. needs China and vice versa, so there is a definite love-hate relationship developing between the two super powers. This quote seems to surmise the current climate, and adds an interesting twist to the debate.

"Most recently, the cyclical stagnation in Washington for a viable bipartisan solution over a federal budget and an approval for raising debt ceiling has again left many nations' tremendous dollar assets in jeopardy and the international community highly agonized," Xinhua said.

The editorial called for "a new world order" in which "all nations, big or small, poor or rich, can have their key interests respected and protected on an equal footing." (Xinhau, 2013)

Now it seems obvious from the quote that China wants the United States to get their fiscal affairs in order. But why on earth would the Chinese be calling for a New World Order? Wouldn't it seem like China would be calling for their sovereignty instead of more globalism? It seems the power elite's tentacles have spread further than originally thought. At some point China will tire of their current investments losing value, and either pull out of the US dollar entirely and switch to other currencies, commodities, crypto currencies, or gold. It is also possible that they will quickly start buying up entire segments of vital US, infrastructure to increase long-term bargaining power. Some of which has already started to happen, over the last few years China has become a major real estate buyer in cities like Detroit and Toledo, Ohio leading many to speculate they are preparing to transfer some of their manufacturing plants back to the U.S. In addition, Chinese companies, of which 60% are owned by the Chinese government, have been buying up large companies like Smithfield foods, the number producer in the U.S. of pork supplies. Although fiscal war is the most likely outcome of all this, we can never eliminate the chance of an out-and-out ground war as well. One never knows what the future may hold, but we can be sure that the paper the Chinese are holding is starting to become virtually worthless. Most of these dollars represent little more than derivative based IOU's, and most of the derivatives' are worth pennies on the dollar. So appropriately, the Chinese are a bit concerned at the moment.

It is obvious that most people don't realize a good thing until it is gone, conversely many people also don't realize a bad thing until it is gone either. The New York Times, a mouthpiece for the globalists feel that the world reserve currency is too big of a burden for the U.S to shoulder alone.

"Third, the dollar's losing reserve status might not be such a bad thing, either for the United States or the world. Today the dollar is hobbled not only by Washington's appetite for self-destruction.

The job of reserve currency is too big for the dollar to shoulder alone. Under the current system, every time some country on the other side of the world wants to add one dollar to its reserves, the United States government must issue one additional dollar worth of debt.

As a recent report about how to reform the world monetary system pointed out, the balance sheet of the United States government is not big enough to accommodate the reserves demanded by the rest of the world. Other currencies — most likely the euro and the Chinese renminbi — must eventually provide feasible alternatives." –Eduardo Porter

The bi-lateral trade agreements have been made by many South American nations to trade in currencies other than dollars as well. Brazil and Argentina are two notable players in this equation. What many Americans fail to realize is the fact that many of these South American countries used to be very prosperous places in times past. Many younger people have never known the South American nations to be anything but third world cesspools, but this is really a recent turn of events. Cuba used to be the Las Vegas of the 1950's. The mafia used Cuba for a lot of racketeering, and money laundering during that time period, so it's sad that we cannot retain these once great economies as trading partners. These bilateral agreements amount too little more, than votes of no confidence in the US political system. It's sad that we can't retain these once great economies as trading partners.

Besides just reinvesting their assets into gold, other countries are also buying up other tangible assets and proven cash cow businesses within the US. China just recently purchased AMC movie theaters; it doesn't get more Americana than movie theaters. But not anymore, now the Chinese own them. Although if you're the United States perhaps it's convenient that the Chinese own AMC, as they will not object to any form of egregious propaganda films that are due for release. China has also been offered deals to buy companies such as Fisker, an electric car company, and Smithfield foods, the largest US pork producer. Sadly the quality of pork will soon get even worse.

"Smithfield Foods Inc. (SFD), the world's largest hog and pork producer, said U.S. regulators will allow the company to be bought by China's Shuanghui International Holdings Ltd. in what would be the biggest Chinese purchase of a U.S. firm.

"This transaction will create a leading global animal protein enterprise," Zhijun Yang, Chief Executive Officer of Shuanghui International, said in a joint statement from both companies released yesterday." (Bloomberg, 2013)

China probably has been made aware that many of their US assets are virtually worthless, but are stuck with them due to the fact that we are their main source of income. So even though they are buying fake money, the US is still giving them real tangible assets from time to time, to fend off the wolves.

Getting out of this cycle of the great US fiscal sell-a-thon, will have to come through either massive policy change, or else a Global Economic Reset. There are no other viable options available. Although the US still has some of the most brilliant minds in the world, we still lack the deep sense of justice and morality that differentiated us from the rest of the dictator/monarch nations worldwide. Having to reset, would not be the end of the world, as the defacto banking dictators, don't seem to be giving up anytime soon. A reset would give smaller Americans a bigger portion of the pie, if we are able to play our hands wisely.

6 The Rise of China and the Eastern Super Bloc

The rise of China is nothing new, after all, they have been building empires way before the English were cuddling up to the Magna Carta. Although their economy was artificially suppressed due to the English control of Hong Kong and the closed economic policies under Mao, times have changed. China has recently been building back up to its pre-Mao economic condition. This growth has happened slowly and steadily over the past 30 years. Most recently China has been moving towards massive infrastructural buildup, and a policy of mass resource accumulation. Year after year, their military expenditures have slowly grown into a force to be reckoned with worldwide. China is doing their best to take the rest of the world by storm, by quietly playing their hand and keeping a low profile. Once in a blue moon you will hear a Chinese general talk about nuclear warfare with some potential threat, but this rhetoric has yet to proliferate into anything meaningful.

As with most geopolitical tough-talk, it generally amounts to a lot of glorified chest pounding, ultimately aimed at scaring the home populations. As badass as they might think they are, it seems like the Chinese are not as economically sophisticated as the black magicians of Wall Street—a group that is never to be underestimated. To some extent you could say that the Chinese have made communism viable long term; a task that many other countries have failed miserably at. Now obviously this is a negative influence worldwide, but it does speak to their advanced methodologies of control--and to their ability to maintain a command-control economy. No matter how you slice it, China will be a force to be reckoned with in the next 20 years.

The Chinese currency the Rembinmi is severely undervalued in comparison to the dollar, and has created a very sensitive political landscape. Tensions have definitely run high since China has been refusing to raise the value of its currency, and also refuses to purchase many goods from the United States.

"Here's an encouraging figure from last year about the imbalanced U.S.-China economic relationship: American exports increased to a record $110 billion, a gain of 6.2% from 2011. The

wide range of U.S. companies that doing business to China include Boeing BA -1% and Harley-Davidson HOG -2.37%.

The trouble was on the import side. Even though exports increased, the overall U.S. trade deficit with China expanded to $315 billion because of imports grew by a higher 6.6%, to $425 billion, or almost four times as much as the U.S. sells. That big drain tends to slow U.S. economic growth at a time when our government debt is huge and unemployment is high." (Flannery, 2014)

It seems that China is playing their own version of monetary monopoly, by attempting to consolidate their position, by gobbling up currencies worldwide. To do what with one might ask? This is anyone's guess, but military aggression seems to be high on the list. One has to wonder what lies in the incubator of the Chinese power structure.

It came out recently that China had racked up a massive 1.37 trillion US dollars, almost surpassing the all-time high. China has single handedly financed the war In Iraq and Afghanistan, as the total cost of both wars at this point is approximately 1.5 trillion.

One of the best sites to review such information is this. (National

Priorities, 2014)

It gives you a break down up to this minute of spending costs...

It is strange that the insanely large derivative bubble has not really affected Chinese US Treasury bill purchases. One would have to wonder if there was another strategy being implemented behind the scenes. Despite what might be happening in backroom deals, on the surface China is financing the US more aggressively than ever...

"The $1.317 trillion figure exceeds China's previous record high in July 2011 of $1.315 trillion, according to the government data. China's appetite for government debt has been driven by its huge amount of foreign-exchange reserves, which surged to a record of $3.82 trillion at the end of 2013. The demand for Treasury's does not appear to have been seriously eroded by concerns about the U.S. fiscal situation." (Fox Business, 2014)

China's thirst for a massive infrastructural buildup can best be seen by looking at the insane spike of copper prices--copper is one of the core raw materials used in building systemic infrastructure. The Wall Street Journal recently noted how just such a spike has continued, despite industry predictions of a slowdown due to Chinas sluggish economy.

"Surprisingly strong Chinese copper demand is prompting investors to rethink their dour predictions for the metal.

Copper consumption by the world's biggest user remains resilient even as China's economy cools and Beijing attempts to tighten access to credit, analysts say. Stockpiles of the metal in London Metal Exchange warehouses have fallen 50% since late June. Much of that copper has been moving to China, industry experts say." (Wall Street Journal, 2014)

China has also been quietly building up their armed forces as well. This is on the heels of some hard talk about contesting islands in the region off of the south pacific. They seem to be feeling a bit more confident, and have ramped up warfare capabilities considerably.

"However, there is one generally agreed explanation for their prominence: The PLA now has something to talk about. The military budget has soared to almost $200 billion, according to some Western estimates - the world's second-highest military budget behind the United States. That money has paid for the

warships; strike aircraft and missiles allowing the PLA to plan for distant conflict. For the first time in its modern history, China has the firepower to contest control of disputed territory far from its coastal waters." - (Lague, 2014)

It's hard to say exactly what their nuclear capacity is, but it is known that china has a very large network of underground bases. I would imagine this is a common strategic outlook for many militaries worldwide.

"While Barack Obama is busy gutting the U.S. nuclear arsenal, Russia and China are rapidly preparing for the day when they will nuke the United States. To most Americans, it sounds very strange to hear that Russia and China are concerned about nuclear war. After all, isn't the Cold War over? Isn't that what politicians from both major political parties keep telling us? Unfortunately, the truth is that Russia and China both consider the United States to be their number one geopolitical threat, and both nations have been systematically strengthening and updating their strategic forces. At the end of last month, Russia held a large-scale military drill that involved the launch of four

nuclear missiles, and the Chinese government released a major

report for the public, which included maps showing what would

happen to major U.S. cities in the event of a nuclear attack by

Chinese submarines. Obama may blindly believe that wishful

thinking and unilateral disarmament will keep the United States

safe, but Russia and China are taking a much different path.

Both of them believe that a military conflict with the United

States in the future is quite likely, and they are rapidly preparing

for that eventuality." (Freedom Outpost, 2013)

Another good article about the tension in the South China Sea can be
found here:

(http://www.bloomberg.com/news/2013-06-18/china-s-military-
buildup-worrisome-japan-s-u-s-ambassador-says.html)

One such general commented that China is prepared to accept
the survival scenarios of nuclear war, and begin living underground.
Obviously this seems drastic and dystopic, but I guess when you're
financing a mega power broker empire such as the United States you
need to be prepared for anything. (Environmental Graffiti, 2014)

As recently as March of 2013 the state department hosted a general Zhu of China, who had threatened nuclear war on the United States. One would wonder where the true allegiances lie in this country if we are inviting these people over for a cookout at the Whitehouse.

Zhu is best known for inflammatory comments made to two foreign news reporters in 2005 when he said China would use nuclear weapons against the United States in any conflict over Taiwan.

A State Department spokesman at the time called the comments "highly irresponsible."

"If the Americans draw their missiles and position [sic]-guided ammunition onto the target zone on China's territory, I think we will have to respond with nuclear weapons," Zhu told reporters for the Financial Times and the Asian edition of the Wall Street Journal, according to their July 14, 2005, editions." – (Gertz, 2014)

It's hard to say where exactly China stands with the United States at this point, but with them threatening to attack everyone in their localized region, you can be assured that the engines of war are alive and well, and that things are not going to be totally quiet on that side of the world for the next decade or so. The United States has quietly made enemies with the entire world by hyper inflating the world's money supply. Soon everyone in the eastern and western worlds will come to realize just how worthless a non-gold-backed fiat currency can become over time. It's anyone's guess how China will respond when they figure out the 1.37 trillion US dollars isn't worth much at all. The only thing you can be sure of is a fair amount of outrage. Who would not be mad after figuring out that such an insane amount of money wasn't worth the paper it was printed on? We might as well have shipped over a trillion continentals over there, perhaps then they would at least have some sort of nostalgic value. My guess is in the next five to fifteen years, everyone will be treating the current fiat Washington dollars like continentals. Perhaps we need some rebranding, or the dollar might become a term of the past.

The Russians have also been getting all snuggly with China as well, quietly making trade alliances, and trying to form an international wedge to protect themselves from US hegemony. Again they are in close proximity for them to want to make a solid front, thereby limiting the ability for the US to conduct any boots on the ground type intimidation tactics across the Pacific. They have been conducting many joint military exercises, and making trade alliances, that again point towards the demise of the Petro dollar. It is also rumored that is was the Russians who gave the Chinese the recipe for forming nuclear weapons. Although Bill Clinton also gave the Chinese plans to many of our US nuclear reactors during his first term.

The next likely scenario is that China will emerge with their own form of a world reserve currency, thereby forcing the US's hand, and creating a major supply line problem for US companies nationwide. As if it were not for cheap Chinese imports, the US economy, and in particular the retail sector will all but grind to a halt. Again it will cost the Chinese a lot of money to do that, but at least they have the infrastructure to rebuild after a collapse, where the United States does not. All of our vital infrastructure is dilapidated and dying, and our industrial manufacturing is almost non-existent.

7 Three Scenarios for the Global Economic Reset

Authors note: For the sake of brevity in this chapter we will contain our discussion on hypotheticals to the United States for the time being, as every country has a pretty unique relationship with protests and with governmental change, so attempting to analyze the global effects outside of a strictly currency context would be a very elongated affair.

Up to this point in human history, it may be safe to surmise that perhaps sanity is not exactly a renewable resource. As typical for megalomaniacs, the powers that be have decided that it's better to wreck everything, so that control can be maintained. Controlling everything from mega yachts or underground bunkers worldwide is the surface goal it would seem--being that ecocide is happening around every corner. Everything has its price, and you may be able to sell your soul to keep things afloat for a while, but eventually these long-term imbalances will be rectified.

Humanity, although not an entirely benevolent race of beings, is a race full of potential. If one thing is clear, it's that our duty as human beings is to, day-after-day, year-after-year, struggle to become better people. If we're not striving for something, then what are we here for? Striving for what you ask? Well that depends on the purpose of your life, and if you don't know that, then I can't tell you. For that is something you must find within yourself. Once you find the unique purpose of your life, you must hold on to it like as if it were the most precious jewel of your existence. Without purpose, a human being is a supremely sad creature to observe.

You need not venture further than your local dive bar to find recurring purposelessness in action. Day after day, drink after drink, the masses search in vain, hoping to find purpose at the bottom of a bottle. On the other hand, it is an inherent joy to bear witness to the purpose directed, self-asserted human being who creates his meaning daily. A being that exhibits to the world, that with every action they take, there is a sense of destiny to accompany it. A person of true meaning, couldn't live their life any other way. These types of warriors against conformity and restriction are existentially unassailable. You may kill them, but you will never touch their spirit. They are stronger than they look, unperturbed by the hollow pageantries' society has to offer. Comfortable behind the scenes when necessary, living as if they will live forever--viewing death as a companion, not as an adversary. Death does not only come as a physical phenomenon. Death also happens psychologically. This type of death is actually more important on many levels, as it is the prime driver of meaningful self-development. Without this form of death, morality might be lost to the world. This type of psychological subconscious change allows humanity to avoid past mistakes, while building a more psychically hygienic future.

In order for us to get a better grasp on the multitude of changes that accompany a global economic reset of this magnitude, I have assembled what I consider to be the three most likely scenarios in which this fiscal bubble will pop. Allowing us to glean into the good the bad, and the ugly of the Global Economic Reset.

1. Fiscal Sanity is Restored

To be clear, it should be noted that this is the best-case scenario, and this option is still very possible. If this scenario ends up playing out, America could re-enact all of the laws that could have prevented this nonsense from happening in the first place. These measures include reinstating Glass Stiegel, returning to the gold standard, and making way for competing currencies. Granted the transitional period would be rough, and may last 10-15 years. Even the best-case scenario would inevitably cause a period of severe economic depression for those dependent upon government social security, Medicare, and Medicaid. Yet if you were free from those governmental systems, you would likely be able to get by unscathed.

During its golden years, America had record-breaking levels of double digit domestic GDP growth, this happened while we were using a variety of sound currencies. The world would obviously be receptive to the return of a moral United States economy, instead of the evil empire that currently exists. If we just leveled with countries worldwide, and told them that all dollars were effectively worthless, they might be willing to negotiate--especially if they could be exchanged for gold, or equity in a new form of sound currency. Countries might still be up in arms, but really what could they do? Fight us using our own currency? I highly doubt they would be able to surmount the debt bubble any better than we could. As it stands now, it seems like many countries are just trying to be the last economy standing, and at the higher levels the bankers know that this system is doomed. With regard to this bubble, the whole world, is in for a world of pain.

Although, if we look at what happened in Iceland just a few years ago, we can glean an understanding into how this best-case scenario would play out. First there were some protests out in the streets, and then they recompiled the legitimate financial ledgers of the whole nation. Then they ended up arresting many of the fiscal henchmen behind the Icelandic fake debt derivatives bubble. Iceland was able to stave off economic disaster, and turn the ship around within a year's time; all while barely missing any work in the process. That process is detailed below.

"Iceland's peaceful revolution is a stunning example of how little our media tells us about the rest of the world. (Daily Kos, 2011)

"The lesson to be learned from Iceland's crisis is that if other countries think it's necessary to write down debts, they should look at how successful the 110 percent agreement was here," said Thorolfur Matthiasson, an economics professor at the University of Iceland in Reykjavik, in an interview. "It's the broadest agreement that's been undertaken."

Without the relief, homeowners would have buckled under the weight of their loans after the ratio of debt to incomes surged to 240 percent in 2008, Matthiasson said.

Iceland's $13 billion economy, which shrank 6.7 percent in 2009, grew 2.9 percent last year and will expand 2.4 percent this year and next, the Paris-based OECD estimates. The euro area will grow 0.2 percent this year and the OECD area will expand 1.6 percent, according to November estimates.

Housing, measured as a subcomponent in the consumer price index, is now only about 3 percent below values in September 2008, just before the collapse. Fitch Ratings last week raised Iceland to investment grade, with a stable outlook, and said the island's "unorthodox crisis policy response has succeeded. "An article at Wakeup World says "The Icelandic economy will outgrow the Eurozone in 2012 and is set to outgrow the entire developed world on average, according to estimates from the Organization for Economic Cooperation and Development." (Bloomberg, 2012)

"Now Iceland is proceeding to actually prosecute some of their formerly most powerful bankers and the Icelandic special prosecutor has stated that it very well may indict some 90 people.

Meanwhile, over 200 people, including the former chief executives of Iceland's three biggest banks, face criminal charges for their activities.

ICELAND (GP) – No news from Iceland? Why? Last we heard, people were rising up and overthrowing the bankers. Then, no news on the television or newspapers for two years. What happened? Why won't the papers and TV tell us how the bankers successfully crushed or minimized another rebellion? Because... THEY DIDN'T! This time, the people won." (Crazy Emails and Back Stories, 2012)

Sadly this process would be much more complex for a country like the United States to accomplish. Being that we have 20-30 years' worth of fiscal banking shenanigans to deal with, it would be almost impossible to accurately revalue the economic system. Since derivatives have been bundled into 90% of the mortgages in this country, it makes this type of easy out scenario improbable.

Again to turn this thing around peacefully, we will need the help of a hell of a lot of whistle blowers on Wall Street, within the Federal Reserve, congress, the media, etc. This process has been jumpstarted with the Edward Snowden revelations, but it seems that the whistleblowers from Wall Street have had a much more difficult time trying to go public with their information. It seems as though the 40 plus so called banker "suicides" have been closely linked to the derivatives markets, and the impending financial collapse. Although the bankers might be greedy, many of them still have some sanity left, as they also have families and such. Insider info suggests that many of these "suicides" were from bankers who were industry insiders trying to blow the whistle on the inside baseball regarding the casino culture of Wall Street and the central banks. The bankers realize that once there is no more trust in the dollar, the jig is up, and they will all be forced to live out the hard reality of a central banking dictatorship. At the end of the day, very few people really want that scenario to happen. Once that happens its game over for the Wall Street free-for-all.

People need to be told the truth of the situation, and that isn't going to happen easily. Most people don't care for the truth, and much prefer living in personal bubbles of existence, and to some extent; who can blame them? Lying is a hard habit to break, as anyone who lied, as a kid will know. A lot of the reforms would need to come from a legitimate three branch of government Republic like we used to have in America, not a government bought and paid for by the banking cartels and central planners--but as anyone knows, the current system is a illegitimate bloated piece of junk. At this point our system does little more than keep the criminals in charge, and out of jail. So relying on them is a real long shot, especially since many of the Supreme Court justices are doing a piss poor job on defending even basic civil liberties. Baby steps will be the name of the game; going back to a few different regionalized competing currencies would help a lot. Not to mention jailing all of the bankers that caused this total economic mayhem. Although all of these reforms are possible, it's represents an unlikely option, as the systemic collapse will most likely have to happen first.

The pivotal point will come when the collapse does come. Will we handle it with dignity and sanity? Or will we start robbing our neighbors and grandma for the jar of peanut butter? Sadly there will be some in America that fall into the latter category. We must remain morally upright, just; and help to manage distress in a spiritually based, and emotionally grounded way. Panic leads to poor planning and hasty decisions. If you are inwardly at peace, there is never any reason to panic as you realize that nature provides equally for all of her creatures, and that winter always turns into spring eventually. Otherwise, if we choose to panic, we are doomed to repeat this whole subconsciously based disaster model time after time. As was evidenced in France after the terrible bout with Hyperinflation, the people panicked and it lead to the horror show of the French revolution. A revolution where tens of thousands where guillotined including women and children, not a pretty site.

With creation, mankind had to reckon with the prospect of destruction. Don't fear it! Get to know it, listen to it, for you will need destruction as an ally in just such scenarios. Obviously this does not mean you have to physically kill, or be killed, but you must recognize that things in this reality are impermanent, and some people will have to face harsh consequences for their karmic actions, in order to energetically rectify the situation. For in times of mass upheaval, the criminal bankers and politicians will not be able to retain total control. It becomes a bit of a Pandora's Box scenario that can create major reforms in the blink of an eye. This is how we can create positive change by allowing positive destruction to take place.

2. Total Revolt

Total old school revolution is a possibility if we are met with total and unequivocal fiscal collapse. A revolt would most likely start with the banks shutting off access to money. When people can't use their debit cards, the yuppies will panic, and all Hades will break out. Luckily there are not enough armies in the world to stop the gun toting American populace from shooting people down if they cannot find enough food out in the streets. Although self-defense is always advisable, and total pacifism is a recipe for disaster historically speaking, armed conflicts are to be avoided if at all possible.

More recently, the incident at the Bundy ranch saw tempers flaring in all directions. With the Bureau of Land Management attempting to seize cattle from a 150 year settlement entitled rancher, the Libertarian and patriot movement rushed in to defend Mr. Bundy. Luckily this particular incident did not end in bloodshed, although it was very close to happening. The rancher and armed populace marched against the feds, and were able to effectively force the feds to back down, and release the cattle they had effectively stolen from Mr. Bundy--a tense incident to say the least. It's hard to say what will happen next time a scenario like this happens but it was reassuring to see that some of the American populace still has the cojones to ride up against tanks, and call the Feds bluff.

If a civil war style revolt does start, it will probably be started by the feds staging small staged false-flag events targeting patriot groups. In this case patriot shoot-outs and small or medium size explosives would be the order of the day. This trend would trigger a chain reaction of police stand offs which would spread across the heartland of America. As economic assistance programs break down, people will start taking aim at their local economic treasuries, banks, and stores looking for reparations to replace their social security checks. Perhaps there will also be rogue elements within the military that would try to stage a coup, or perhaps local/state governments are toppled, thereby leading to a small bout of secessionism. However it happens, this would be a pretty ugly option. Millions of Americans would die due to starvation, and from small skirmishes with police and military nationwide. If we look back to the civil war, it should be obvious that this scenario is still entirely possible. It would be hard to predict exactly how the new currency system would emerge in this case, but it would make sense that the economies would need to first find their bearings upon the good old barter system.

It is also interesting to note that the concept of squatter's rights might go back into effect. Which I personally think would make things very interesting, during the great depression squatters rights existed so that if you were not currently at a property it could be commandeered by locals, hence the many mansions of the super rich could be commandeered as temporary living quarters. Think about what many of the radical communists in the Occupy Wall Street movement would do; hells bells! Many of these investment properties, and 2nd homes would make for good living quarters. I mean if the elite are off living in underground bunkers anyways, and shaking in their boots, why would they need them? Now obviously this would only happen in an extreme scenario, but it would be interesting to witness, as it has happened before, and it is happening in limited cases around the country already...

"But just as the recession has put a new spin on the term "underwater" and added "staycation" to our lexicon, it's created

a new class of squatters. After all, squatters used to simply park themselves on a property they'd never paid for and gain rights to it over time by meeting the requirements for a legally sanctioned title snatch and paying property taxes on the parcel. And the recession has certainly given rise to its share of this flavor of squatters. Most real estate brokers who list foreclosed homes these days can tell stories about having to call local cops because a homeless person has moved into a vacant property owned by the bank. There are even many reports of "mansion squatters" trying to snatch legal ownership of foreclosed luxury homes." (Business Time, 2011)

This scenario would also involve a lot of starvation, as the government loves to let people die. Bankers love civilian starvation. As starvation serves to remind the populace how things would be without large government there to prevent such things from happening. Millions died of starvation during the great depression, so it would seem likely that it could happen again. Remember big daddy government needs your consent, as well as your money. Even though America was built upon the promise of freedom for some, it has quickly gone in the exact opposite direction. Revolution is a psychologically-healthy tendency that keeps things honest. Revolution also makes way for new societal innovations that more closely serve the true needs of the people.

This type of revolt would lead to a series of economic shockwaves, as it would severely hamper our world trade abilities, forcing us to become semi-industrialized once again. What would Apple do if it were forced to create iPods and computers inside the United States? The price for such devices would probably be two or threefold, yet if our currency wasn't hyper inflated already it wouldn't be a big deal. As if we had a sound currency we could still afford such a purchase, as our overall purchasing power would definitely be higher. They lead us to believe that we need lots of foreign labor, and foreign support, when the truth is, the United States did just fine when we made most everything here at home. Nobody starved, and people were more appreciative of the things that they did have.

3. Worldwide Digital Enslavement

If the world controllers get their way, this is what the most ruthless of the banking elite would like to see happen. In this version of events, the bankers will shut down every last sector of the economy. They will consolidate complete control within the corridors of their power, and they will switch the whole world onto their global digital currency, in which people do transactions on nothing but crypto currencies. Everyone is issued a number, and if you don't have a currency number, you are unable to interact with the marketplace, and are effectively banished from all further commerce. This will be put into place through the bio-metric ID cards. They could come in the form of a microchip, or perhaps some other form of highly advanced sensors place into a traditional ID. Without that biometric number, you will be forced to go out into tribal third world nations to do business. Effectively shutting you off from major portions of global commerce, and severely limiting your ability to earn a living.

The other possible scenario would entail a form of digital indentured servitude, in which you're forced to serve the elite, in order to buy back your financial autonomy. Once a cashless system, or a biometric system goes into effect, there is not much preventing the digital controllers from limiting the purchasing ability of "select" citizens. Cash, and physical tender, is one of the benchmarks of freedom, and modern societies will need it to keep things from devolving into a post human robotic prison.

In this scenario all hope is lost, as the Trans humanist agenda is complete. All citizens are forced to eventually merge with machines, and one by one, all concepts of freedom, and freewill are turned off--along with all human emotions. You effectively enter into a post human matrix, and lose any chance you once had at individuation, or spiritual union with the higher power of the Universe. Pretty bleak right? Well if we don't wake up and make some serious changes to where things are headed, this is totally possible. You only have to look around for 5 minutes to realize that we are halfway there. People are more attached to their iPhones than to their friends or lovers. When people would rather play with their apps than have sex or hangout with their friends, we know something is pretty askew.

Freedoms are a use it or lose it type of privilege. If you're not constantly vigilant, you will lose all privileges, and become a slave to your own mundane existence. We must always exercise as many freedoms as we possibly can, because if we don't use our freedoms they will be slowly taken away one by one. All the while the range of the human experience will also shrink as well. Turning our planet more and more into a nonsensical subhuman sports worshipping, big brother prostrating, 3rd grade vocabulary level bunch of nincompoops.

Door number 1-3?

Whichever scenario ends up playing out, the whole debate is a double-edged sword. It is hard to say exactly how such a Global Economic Reset would pan out, as this is the most complex world economic system that the world has ever seen. Even with all the supercomputers in the world, modeling this kind of a collapse is not easily done. This is probably why the world controllers have been hesitant to green light such a massive implosion. They will not pull the trigger on such a wide scaled economic collapse unless they are 100% certain that the ball will land in their court. Like we stated earlier, with regards to international currency creation, nothing is left up to chance. A digital trans-humanist takeover of the world would be no different.

The elites worldwide have manufactured mass revolutions of all kinds, somehow retaining their seats of power for thousands of years. These people fit an evil genius arch-type and are never to be underestimated. This multi-headed-hydra will require very sophisticated planning, to dismantle permanently--albeit they are already starting to collapse under their own weight. Brute force alone does nothing; in fact the most powerful tacticians of all time realize that brute force is one of the least effective methods of warfare. The powers that run the international banking syndicate realized long ago just how powerful the ability to coin currency is. The central bankers have proven time and time again that they are willing to kill anyone, or do anything in order to gain control of the money printing apparatus worldwide. This is a key lynchpin to global control, and if we do not reclaim this fundamental ability to create a sound trustworthy currency, we will be doomed to suffer the same fate, time and time again. For ultimately money is just representative of energy, and if we can't control our own psychic creative energy, then we will not be able to build a world in a way that we see fit.

It makes one wonder how a country could ever be free with the existence of a central bank. Had the founders really wanted to sustain our freedom long-term, it seems like they would have issued much stricter regulations of banking--as this has been one of the prime drivers of tyranny throughout the ages.

Until further notice, a policy of global economic warfare is the default agenda, so we must prepare for anything.

8 The Rush to Horde Assets/Too Much Debt in the World

The amazing part about greed, is the non-locality of it. Greed is a universal indisputable phenomenon of global civilization in general. Anytime there is a complex societal structure an indescribable need seems to erupt, for you to collect more stuff than your neighbor has. If we think about this in term of a video game, generally all the video games revolve around collecting items, building cities, and other acquisitive tasks. The masses like these kinds of games because they are an extension of our external circumstances out in the world, therefore we can relate to them on a subconscious level.

It's inherently difficult for people to change and let go. No matter whether that letting go falls within the confines of a hoarder mentality, or in the realm of the global political structures. Back 200-300 years ago, people loved the idea of a king, and not just anywhere but right here in America. They begged and pleaded George Washington to become a king. It was only after a good amount of pushback that he was able to declare that the United States would become a Republican system, instead of a monarchical one. I don't think I have to point out that 300 years ago isn't a very long time, so if you think that the subconscious of humankind has evolved past liking the idea of a big daddy government, you might want to think again.

The fact that the world is hording assets makes sense on one hand, being that we know how it gives people a sense of "safety". Yet when does that safety, become your prison? Hording things can also make countries very vulnerable. As when money stops changing hands, economies slow, and people grow desperate. Who wants to go to work if they know they are not getting paid? With regards to the United States for example, we are so helplessly strung out on oil, that if another country were able to disrupt our supply for an extended period of time, it would make it incredibly difficult for us to defend ourselves in the event of a major war.

Yet economically every country is still going to be in competition to be the biggest and the baddest son-of-a-bitch on the block. So predictably we see the historical pissing matches continue unabated, and perhaps for good reason--as competition is one of the main drivers of human achievement. Without the occasional bout of friendly competition, how would you know what your true potential was?

Within humanity lies an inherent drive for uniqueness. We all have aspirations to be the best at something, and perhaps a desire to explore where no other has gone before. This again leads us back to the human fascination with video games and other virtual realities. In these games, we are the best, we are the hero, we are the savior, and we are the God creature. Video games represent what we know we could be, if we could just muster the courage to let go. Sadly video games inspire anything but letting go, they keep us stuck in fixed patterns, viewing some external character as the hero. Letting us play out fantasies in a semi unhealthy way. They represent a way that does not give true outlet to our deeper emotions and desires, as nature would. Instead they keep us enthralled in digital utopias.

In my view, the amount of debt in the world is actually akin to how much we feel we owe ourselves for spiritual self-masochism of our species. Debt is represents nothing more than the amounts of energy that we have subconsciously stolen from ourselves. Obviously personal philosophies and metaphysics play a role in this equation, but I will leave that up to the reader to ponder. Yet instead of creating jobs to build the planet into a better world, we have chosen to pay ourselves for the planets self-destruction. What a concept right? What other creature in nature would attempt to create money out of thin air, and then convince the rest of the world that they owed trillions of dollars in fictional money. Just stop and think about how insane that is. This seems to me like a game of monopoly gone horribly wrong, at this point we will be lucky to keep Baltic Ave.--if we keep playing by their rules!

The brass tacks of the situation is this, there is just as much matter on the earth as there was 10 million years ago, and no economic system will be able to create or destroy more matter than was already in existence. In real terms, the earth will always have the exact same amount of money available. We just need to decide on a better way to utilize it. If we can really try to cooperate and build something beautiful then our souls may grow in the process of some economic transformation. But if we are stuck in acquisitiveness, we won't ever be able to find our higher calling. Material stuff is just material stuff, there's nothing inherently good or bad about it. It all comes from earth, water, metal, air, and fire. Nothing is beyond the alchemical process of our reality. The sooner we realize that these wars are fought in a vain attempt to hold gallons of water in the palm of one's hand, the better off we will be. We can only allow the money (aka the water) to flow into the proper channels on its own accord. If we try to dam the river up and horde the water, then all we do is damn ourselves--literally and figuratively speaking.

The true free market economy with competing currencies represents one of the only ways to restore true sanity to our lives. We have been beat over the head with socialism for so long that many people no longer realize what true capitalism looks like. Hell even in the 1930's true capitalism was a dying thing within the major urban metropolitan areas, as the mafia had already taken over large swaths of major industry. This system eventually spawned into today's crony capitalist rigged market. The generation growing up in today's media climate is even more entranced with socialism. Until this generation wakes up to the true economic scams happening, they will have a tough road to hoe. Luckily many of the younger ones are bucking the system, which is a positive sign. Capitalism had a great run from 1776-1910 or so, after that we have been inching ever closer to a socialist gluttonous government run economy.

Deep down people worldwide understand that the current economic modalities are totally unsustainable, as is evidenced by the Chinese rushing to come in and buy up many precious tangible assets all over the US and abroad. The elites and power brokers alike, know that whoever retains the hard assets, will usually be the victor in an economic collapse. Every instance of hyperinflation, has led to resurgence in real tangible assets being the currency of choice. Things like Gold, Silver, real estate, mineral rights, indentured populations, and tactical military positions become methods of domination in these scenarios.

As noted in previous chapters, the race for countries to horde physical precious metals has officially begun. Many countries are quickly realizing that the gold being kept by the U.S. Federal Reserve banks is not exactly in safe hands. Many other countries also believe that much of this gold has been sold out from under their noses, to other foreign buyers, and most of it is gone. Germany recently asked to have their gold holdings repatriated. This was at first met with a total stonewalling by the US Treasury, but finally after much posturing, they finally responded. In the response they stated that yes, Germany could have its gold back, but it would take 7-8 years to return it. If that's not some kind of a scam I don't know what is. All that there seems to be is conjecture at this point over what gold and precious metal reserves are actually left at this point. All that can be known for sure is that there is a lot of strange activity happening in this department, and if you want to get your billion worth of gold out of one of the mega banks, you might need to take a number.

"The financial world was shocked this month by a demand from Germany's Bundesbank to repatriate a large portion of its gold reserves held abroad. By 2020, Germany wants 50% of its total gold reserves back in Frankfurt—including 300 tons from the Federal Reserve. The Bundesbank's announcement comes just three months after the Fed

refused to submit to an audit of its holdings on Germany's behalf. One

cannot help but wonder if the refusal triggered the demand.

Either way, Germany appears to be waking up to a reality for which

central banks around the world have been preparing: the dollar is no

longer the world's safe-haven asset and the US government is no longer

a trustworthy banker for foreign nations. It looks like their fears are well-

grounded, given the Fed's seeming inability to return what is legally

Germany's gold in a timely manner. Germany is a developed and

powerful nation with the second largest gold reserves in the world. If

they can't rely on Washington to keep its promises, who can?" – (Schiff,

2014)

As it turns out the modern day banker gold rush does not end there. Ecuador, Romania, Venezuela, and the Dutch are all looking to take control back of their own gold. Striking a cord at the heart of the central bankers. For if we can briefly revisit the Nixon Shock incident, that put us onto a purely fiat system—we will realize that Nixon's political strategy was designed to prevent just such a scenario. At the time in the 1970's, Nixon and the bankers were worried that everyone would pull their gold out of the United States, leaving us high and dry.

So I can imagine that it is safe to assume, the bankers are not happy about returning anyone's gold.

Perhaps the old slogan does apply to world governments..."He who has the gold, makes the rules." I should also mention that gold is not the only asset being horded worldwide. The United States seems to be leading the competition to horde underground bases. America has been building these huge underground bunkers since at least World War 2, and doesn't seem to be slowing down... There are over 120 underground bases in America alone; you can see a list of suspected bases compiled here:

(http://educate-yourself.org/dc/undergroundbaseslisted08feb04.shtml)

Along with bases, countries seem to be stocking oil, natural gas, drugs, and they don't forget the tee pee! China, and Russia are also fast at work in this department, which we noted earlier in Chapter 5. Will someone slap me when all of this is over? Military assets seem to be high on the list of things to horde, otherwise, who would have fun playing GI Joe during economic collapse?

As strange as it seems, ultimately the global financiers actually fear themselves the most. So naturally their actions would include these psychotic fear based hording mentalities. For if you can't trust yourself, who can you trust? Somehow being able to destroy the entire world at the push of a button helps them to sleep better at night. So much for bedtime stories, apparently the big bad wolf does PCP and lives in an elite underground base. The hording of assets is generally a physical thing. Since the bankers can print unlimited amounts of paper money, there's really no reason to hoard that.

Sadly the digital trash heap of international fiat debt goes on for as far as the eye can see. If you are interested in the economic backend of this illusory system and why this amount of debt can never be repaid. Please see some hard facts here: (http://realcurrencies.wordpress.com/2013/04/01/is-there-enough-money-to-pay-off-debt-plus-interest-a-closer-look/)

Regardless of what magic bullet the economists want to pull out of their hat, managing a controlled collapse, and funneling the true resources into another contrived system is something that the central bankers have become very good at over the years, as they have done it hundreds of times historically. Although it may seem outwardly that everyone enters into a period of chaos during such times, this is not the case. Behind the scenes there are the powers that be, waiting to usurp every last little bit of true wealth from the economy, and leave the American public high and dry.

We can think of this in terms of the movie the Matrix, in which the machines who control the planet create their own opposition, by creating a dream world for the humans to live in, which will help to sustain the machine empire. Still at a certain point the machines know that the system has to end, and must be reborn. This is where the bankers find themselves today, faced with the destructive decision to have to implode their own creation, to retain control. Although they don't seem all that worried on the surface, who knows what goes on behind closed doors? Perhaps they are totally ready; perhaps they are not, only time will tell.

Kill or be killed, destroy or be destroyed, the evil that breeds systems like this deal in the souls of man. The farther we go down this road, the more souls that will be lost into the abyss of materialism. Once a man shuts down his spiritual self for good, rebuilding something valuable within becomes much more difficult. So in that sense, it's probably best we have a collapse, before the psyche of man gets too far

down into the psychological.

9 Wars and the Global Economic Reset

War is the quintessential political distraction that the central planners use when looking for causes to current economic crises. Although on one front some claim that war is good for business the truth is just the opposite. War is a massive misallocation of capital that could otherwise be used towards a productive means instead of a destructive one. I think even more than that it is a psychological bleed out from the psychosis of greed worldwide. As reality would have it, war is actually terrible, for most everyone except for the military industrial complex. For the remaining few that still use critical thinking it begs the question... Has the war in Iraq or Afghanistan helped anyone you know? It definitely has not helped anyone that I know. It has only created more death, debt, and overseas mayhem and after spending trillions in Iraq today we see the country melting down with a good possibility of a greater regional war breaking out between the Sunni and Shia. Perhaps this is exactly what the military industrial complex wants, creating environments that lead to the perpetual war state. As the saying goes, easy come easy go. Any short-term gains realized for the government will come at the price of long-term losses--inflation being the primary source of these long-term losses. Although earth is an inherently competitive place, there is plenty for all to share. No one thinking at things from a rational state of mind would feel that warfare is a good way to sustain long-term economic growth. Yet here we are time, and time again; America gets drawn into ambiguous conflicts with no clear enemy or objectives to speak of. Continuously hunting down some boogie man, under a rock somewhere overseas.

Other historical groups have followed these same types of battle tactics. In those days, they were referred to as pirates. The Nordic peoples of the earth used the rape and pillage strategy quite successfully for hundreds of years. At the end of the day I guess it comes down to lifestyle choices, morality, and leadership. At some point you just have to figure out whom exactly you want to decide your fate for you. If you don't have any qualms about stealing your days keep, there is probably a pirate ship in Somalia with your name on it.

Sadly for the Vikings and pirates out there, this model of economic development isn't exactly sustainable. For once you have used up all of the resources from the most recent pillaging, you then have to go out and steal some more. It's really an exhausting way to make a living. While living the Viking lifestyle you are always running a risk of death by arrow, bullet, sword, dysentery, or even worse drowning out on the high seas in the middle of a storm. This is where American military currently finds itself, in the role of the robber baron of the world, assisting the good old UK in re-establishing the global empire, for the name of living up the good life forever.

Predictably the American taxpayers are left with the bill for this whole Viking Hoo-Rah nonsense. The globalists go around the world, and destroy the good name of the average Joe on the street abroad. It's like we are living in a public relations hell, and getting attacked on all sides. All the while, the bankers are fixated on destroying this once great nation through a perpetual hyperinflation--gradually robbing every single man, woman, and child, in this country of their hard earned wages. Hyperinflation also has the convenient effect of destroying the middle class. If taxes are so high that someone making $60,000 per year is actually only making $35,000 that person is effectively no longer considered middle class. Not to mention the fact that there purchasing power with that same $35,000 slowly dwindles lower year after year.

You might be saying, "Well, the Pirates and the Vikings lived their lives to the fullest, and always had a bit of decadence around them." Well perhaps the leaders of these packs had such a lifestyle, but for the average grunt, life probably was much worse than you would imagine. Let's just say the Pirates and Vikings of old were not invited to many dinner parties. They were feared and cursed by common people the world over; known mostly for their brutality, and debauchery.

This is the position America finds itself in. America is in desperate need of a public relations makeover worldwide. Until we recover our good name, other countries will remain hesitant to invest here, and the American people will be left holding the bag. The orchestration of these types of economic war-games is very convoluted and complex; and the hyper-genius nihilists planning all of this are not to be underestimated. Yet ultimately if you continue on our journey of self-discovery, we will come out on top. As Sun Tzu states in the Art of War.

> "If you know the enemy and know yourself, you need not fear the result of a hundred battles. If you know yourself but not the enemy, for every victory gained you will also suffer a defeat. If you know neither the enemy nor yourself, you will succumb in every battle." (Tzu, 1792)

As within chess; any great chess player will be tell you that you need to be thinking 10 moves ahead. The next move is only one action in a chain reaction that will determine the outcome of the game. Social planners, good and evil, are always planning years in advance--figuring out the next strategic point to achieve their end goals.

The War on Hugs....I mean Drugs

"Another "war" we must look into to glean further insight; "The War on Drugs". Officially America's war on drugs began in the late 1800's with the advent of the opium addict. Even though we had already been planting tobacco, hemp, and cocaine to fund the American war efforts, apparently the American profiteers realized there is money in making things illegal. America had already been friendly to tobacco, and strong drink, but never had its shores seen the depths of a hazardous narcotics addiction. As sad as it may seem, drug trade is another main engine of the world economy, and thereby has produced notable advances within both the technological and medicinal fields. For better or for worse, having that much money involved in any industry will produce new inventions and ideas of all sorts. Much

of America's car enthusiast culture came from illegal car modifications that were designed to outrun modern police cars of the time, to aid in delivering drugs and bootlegging. In modern times, we have learned that the Columbians have started building their own fleets of submarines to transport cocaine via the sea floor". (Slate, 2013)

In 1827, Merck a multinational drug company, originally based out of the Germany, developed the first version of morphine, little more than the refined version of Opium, which it began to distribute worldwide for "medical and recreational use". A few years later in 1895 another drug company, Bayer pharmaceuticals, (we might know them for their modern day work distributing aspirin) out of Germany invented Heroine; worldwide addiction quickly ensues. (PBS, 2014) Henceforth one may surmise that drugs are intimately linked with economics, or at least they have been for the past few hundred years.

Drugs and Crypto Currencies

An area generating much buzz within the currency markets has been the advent of crypto currencies. This is where we can look for further insights of what the trends may be going forward. New websites called dark markets have started popping up all over the Internet. You can think of these websites as a sort of an eBay for drugs. They are an anonymous place for users to purchase illegal goods of any sort, while protecting their identities from prying eyes. The biggest such market to date was known as Silk Road; the past tense denotation is due to the fact that this market was shut down by the Feds in October of 2013. The Silk Road dark market had facilitated millions of dollars in drug related transactions using the crypto currency known as Bitcoin. Bitcoin is one of over 300 crypto currencies in existence the first wave of what some think will become the leading competitor to the gold and silver markets as a way for investors to hedge their bets from a collapsing U.S. dollar.

Ultimately history shows the trend of smaller currencies cropping up during tumultuous markets. When markets are left to their own devices they have a natural balancing mechanism. These smaller currencies are also an excellent way to expand trade. This trend showed up prominently during the 17th and 18th centuries with the formation of many smaller merchant currencies developing throughout the period of the enlightenment in Europe. This helped to deflect the amount of risk each individual currency had to bear, and distributed the power base of currencies more equally.

Another dark market website called Sheep marketplace was recently shut down after a hacking theft of 5 million dollars' worth of Bitcoins took place. Obviously stability in the online crypto banking world is still lacking to some degree. It would seem like common sense to the outsider that such a shady drug-dealing marketplace would have its fair share of risks. But it just goes to show that people are willing to sink millions of dollars into untested ideas, in hopes that they can avoid governmental restrictions. Ultimately, it is this instability which will limit the worldwide use of such an economic instrument. Without an army to back it up, and something tangible to take away, it's hard to say that such a string of numbers has any inherent value.

Historically currency has needed to be more tangible to produce peace of mind, but then again peasants during the dark ages used to buy "relics"; these relics were supposed to absolve one of sin and guarantee one access into heaven. People would spend thousands of dollars for small pieces of wood that were supposedly part of the cross from Jesus' crucifixion. All in the hopes that they would be absolved of their sins, and given a one way ticket to a rosy afterlife. Perhaps a sucker is born every minute?

Crypto currency does have some legitimate ideals behind it, and a pretty un-crackable combination to every dollar that it distributes, it's still a bit of a long shot. The lack of banker control, and lack of an army to help enforce some sort of regulations, will probably leave most investors gun-shy. Long-term viable alternative to dollars, have yet to emerge, but I would imagine that they are not far off. As a short-term profit mechanism though, it seems to be a good bet. Knowing when to get out is another story entirely. (History Learning Site, 2014)

"A sucker is born every minute," as they say. This article also well surmises a couple of the fundamental issues with bit coin in its current incarnation.

"Money does three things. It serves as a unit of account; you can quote prices for common goods in dollars, as can all the other people in America. It serves as a store of value, as with the dollars in your bank account. It serves as a medium of exchange; your grocery store takes dollars—and so do you, from your employer.

Bitcoin, like gold and silver, is finite, making it a good store of value. It exchanges well—magnificently, in fact, far better than gold. The way that the Bitcoin protocol uses distributed computing power to verify transactions at a distance is an innovation that has been wanting since the first bills of exchange were offered in the long-distance Mediterranean Sea trade.

VIDEO: Bitcoin Isn't Alone: Newer Currencies Popping Up

Bitcoin is a store of value and a medium of exchange. It's like really awesome gold. It's not, however, a unit of account. Your mother cannot quote you the price of eggs in Bitcoin. This is not just a question of waiting long enough for your mom to get around to using Bitcoin. The state has tremendous power over the unit of account. It pays government contracts in the unit of its choosing. It collects taxes in that unit, too. The psychological weight of this power can last for centuries. Medieval Europe still accounted for its variety of coins in Roman units. Modern Europe uses the metric system because Napoleon wanted it so. It's not clear why any state would choose to give this up.

The Internet beat up publishing and a couple of other industries. It's having a harder time so far against the state. A currency is an asset with an army. Bitcoin has no army. – (Green, 2013)

America has assumed the position of the global-in-laws, no one
wants' them around, yet no one has the balls to give them the boot! We
went from the breadbasket of the world to global gunrunners and petty
drug dealers. Now I have no illusions about the foundations of this
country. Cocaine production was one of our main exports in the late
1700s and 1800s, as well as ordinary hemp. Opium smuggling had also
become a pastime of Americans, as addiction spread like a plague
through England and America alike. The ruling class had found their new
piggy bank with the "War on drugs". Just to illustrate how ruthless this
cabal is, you should know that hemp production was later banned by
the petro chemical industry. This was done in order to shut down the
small farmers, whose land would only support hemp, not cotton, or
other more rigorous crops that required more fertile soil. Shutting down
the little guy for no reason is something that always has to be kept
under constant watch.

Bottom line when the cost for foreign countries to keep their
investments in dollars becomes less than the cost of going to war with
us, then the wars will begin. Many people might ask, "Why would
someone fight a war over money?" Well why else have wars been
fought, other than for power control and utter domination? Some might

also say that wars have been fought for religious reasons, which are true to an extent; but money and power are always lurking closely behind religions.

Religions serve as just one more mode of control over the modern world. Wars are always convenient distractions to misdirect political unrest towards an external enemy. All the while the enemy has been within the city gates the whole time. Now obviously some circumstances exist where warfare is necessary to an extent. Anyone who has read the art of war knows this, and knows that the ultimate objective of warfare should be the preservation of human life. Using warfare for anything besides this is an egregious offense to human life and should be treated as such. Sadly the global banking syndicate has quite a different opinion on these matters, and does not like to mince words with naysayers to their absolutist power driven policies.

War is a long-term fight. Conflict has plagued our species since the beginning of the ages at least. We are fortunate enough to be able to once and for all begin determine the prime factors that fuel the global banking factions. How they operate, why they use both sides against each other, and how they like to keep everyone in the dark and fighting with one another to deflect attention, and control political debates. This is a critical juncture within the human species to strike at the root of the issues facing mankind, instead of merely treating the symptoms as we have done in times past. Deep down money can be traced psychologically to the flow of energy, some cultures equate it to water, to evil, and still others trace it to mechanisms of control.

Whatever someone's personal beliefs might be money is one of the driving forces of all human civilization, and without sound money, social, the result is that cultural progress will be affected. No one has control of the fortune surrounding money more than us. We give power to the systems by buying into them, so can we also tear them down when they no longer serve our needs. As painful as deconstruction may be, it is the single most necessary step in true reform, and people need to be comfortable letting go of the old, to make way for the new!

The global planners know that warfare can serve their agendas on multiple fronts, this is why we are seeing the gross prodding of Russia via the Ukraine right now. If the New World Order oligarchs are to be successful in reorganizing a new currency, or a new form of control in the east, they will first need to tame Russia and China. Both

Russia and China know that they are under great threat from the west, and if nothing is done, there will be a lot of problems to be faced on their doorstep in the coming years. Hard times seem to have arrived at Russia's doorstep, and although their military is quite prepared to deal with these small regional conflicts, they are still not trying to exacerbate the conflict unnecessarily, and get drawn into a resource depleting globalist proxy war. With a country they used to own no less. Russia is playing their hand well, but the globalists are doing everything they can to stir up a small, but sustainable war in the region.

There is always the possibility of the Middle East or China getting involved as well, which would effectively turn this small conflict into more of a WW3 type of scenario, and I can assure you that this is the wet dream of the central planners and the military industrial complex alike. The arms buildup within Chinese and Russian borders is no accident. You don't usually build machines of war, unless you plan to put them to use. The question remains, who these guns will be pointed towards, and how will that serve to restructure the economic system?

Whether the US goes to war with China, Iran, Syria, Russia, or North Korea, the fact remains the same. War remains a massive global diversion, and a way to keep the populace occupied with war activities, and politically disempowered. Chinas currency is also becoming much more popular with trade deals worldwide, so this is also mixing things up. Nothing pisses off a globalist, like getting cut out of a banking deal.

10 The Global Economic Reset

As futile as some of the scenarios laid out may seem; our world is largely comprised of dreams and intangibles; as such anything is possible, even the recreation of a worldwide economic system. In fact if the economic crisis forces people to act out of moral rectitude and dignity, there is no doubt it will become a blessing in disguise. As we all know; without struggle the human species can become an obstinate and lethargic creature. Remaining devoid of morality, and clinging to every last addiction possible to avoid facing the truth about himself. Sometimes catastrophe must strike before they get up off their duff and do something about it. If that's what it takes for people to respond, then so be it. It's not anyone's job to run around and save everyone else. Granted helping people and preaching common sense are always a freewill choice, but we must not become dependent on other peoples spiritual evolving for us to become happy. If we do that, we enslave others to our ideologies, and enslave ourselves to their lack of growth.

Cycles like these just become a yo-yo effect where no one ever gets anywhere meaningful. So on this grand galactic quest for personal reformation of the global economic markets, remember that people can assist the world, but no one man alone will save it. We need to accept things as they are and move on. Hope and optimism are nice qualities, but cultivating actual skills, such as an indubitable work ethic, and a firm sense of long term vision are much nicer than wishing. Wishing is what little kids do--planning, and self-cultivation should be the go-to for adults. Let children dream, they are a force within themselves; and they share in the future dreams of the world. They will be forced to plan and cultivate soon enough.

The Quick Fix vs. The Long Haul

One of the main arguments being presented is to go back to a state of competing currencies, while abolishing the Federal Reserve. Effectively we would be opening the books again to the American people. Now many people on the streets would say this seems like a radical and zany idea, but in fact, as previously discussed it's already happened numerous times throughout world history; most notably after the disillusionment of the fiat "continental currency" debacle. Without competing currencies or gold backed currencies, it's hard to say that any form of power dispersion will be possible within the realm of American economics. As previously stated, Bretton Woods was an agreement that effectively gave the bankers total control over the main monopoly currency (aka the dollar), which effectively turned us back into the continental 2.0. The continental was not backed by anything tangible, nor is the U.S. dollar backed by anything. If we are to recapture the hearts and minds of freedom seekers worldwide, we must too honor capitalist currency competition within our borders. This opinion is garnering more and more headway, as noted by the Forbes writer below, in an incredibly concise article making the case for just such a systematic reform.

> *"The arguments for competing currencies are surely sound. Anything governments can do, profit-motivated private actors can do better, and then it's also the case that history is littered with governments debauching the very currencies they're charged with maintaining in terms of stability. It's certainly true that competition is always a positive and would be for currencies, plus it's not as though private banks haven't historically issued currencies – successfully.*
>
> *And then it's surely true that far from a source of stability, our Federal Reserve is the living embodiment of economic chaos.*

Absent a central bank, it's easy to see where private actors would quickly fill in as lenders of last resort, banks would be better off without Fed oversight that never works to begin with, the economy would no longer suffer a banking system weakened by bailouts or an economy weakened by central bank distorted interest rates, and then even assuming no competing currencies, the Fed's abolishment would almost certainly be a rising dollar event. The dollar is the most important price in the world, so let's get that price out of the devaluationist hands of the Federal Reserve." (Tamney, 2012)

One of my favorite quotes of all time comes from the Classic Think and Grow Rich by Napoleon Hill "Every adversity, every failure, every heart ache carries with it the seed on an equal or greater benefit." Hill also stated, "All the breaks you need in life wait within your imagination. Imagination is the workshop of your mind, capable of turning mind energy into accomplishment and wealth."

This is what we must always bear in mind during the course of any of these crises. It is solely up to us as free thinking entrepreneurial free market capitalists, to go out and create our own fortunes. As Jim

Rome used to say "The same wind blows upon us all." It is up to us to decide if we are going to make a sailboat, or get blown into a ditch. Now does that mean that everyone is going to go out and become 100 % totally self-sufficient, and go live off the land somewhere? No, nor should everyone to go out there and become new age farmers. Now some people are particularly drawn to farming, or horticulture, and good for them. But many people out there probably don't have the least interest in such things, so why go against the grain? Do what seems natural to you, and prepare with pragmatism in mind. When you're going with the flow of events, everything will work itself out in the end. Luckily we live in an age that doesn't require everyone to farm; so don't go buying your plow just yet. Not to mention the fact that farming is a costly investment if you want to start one anywhere near a large city.

The main message here is, do what you love! If you do what you love, or at least something that you have a natural aptitude for, then everyone else will be better off as a result, and you will build value for yourself and your community. The world obviously needs a vast mix of professional talents with which to go round, so contribute in any way you like. If you want to setup a website, or small community based upon bartering, that might be a great idea in the event of a collapse. Until an economic event of some kind does happen, in the meantime people may call you a nut for investing in these things. Yet you will be nuttier your way to the bank if things do get fiscally insane, as everyone will be looking for someone to turn to. A collapse will always create massive opportunities for people prepared to take advantage of the changes within the age. The keys for maintaining a successful business during a collapse are the same as they are at any other time, it requires preparation, patience, analysis, and timing.

Other Competing Currency Alternatives

Most people wouldn't know it, but there are already many forms on competing currencies already thriving on the open marketplace... Forbes Magazine below notes a few of the more popular competing currency examples.

"The most easily recognized complementary currency is frequent flyer miles, now issued by 92 airlines. These do not involve just bonus or discount tickets in return for repeat flight business. "Increasingly, frequent flyer miles are redeemable for a variety of services besides airline tickets, such as long-distance and mobile phone calls, hotels, cruises, and catalog merchandise,"

the authors write. Yet, more than half of frequent flyer miles "are not earned by flying. Instead, credit cards that offer bonus miles with purchases have become the most popular way to earn frequent flyer credits." Consequently, the authors rightly conclude that the frequent flyer miles have "developed into a corporate scrip – a private currency issued, in this case, by airlines."

Another private currency model is time-backed currency, which has been spearheaded by liberal lawyer Edgar Cahn, former advisor to Robert Kennedy and Sergeant Shriver. Participants provide an hour of service to earn an hour of service in return, involving such services as tutoring students, teaching English or other languages, gardening and lawn care, housecleaning, helping the homeless and teaching them skills, rides for those without transportation (or for seniors who can no longer drive), respite care freeing caregivers for children with special needs, adults with disabilities, and aged seniors to take a break, and other services." (Ferrara, 2013)

No Cash? Just Barter.

"Barter services became popular during the Great Depression in the 1930s, which witnessed a scarcity of money. The barter system was used as a way of obtaining things like food and other services. Trading was done between people or through groups, who acted as agents and facilitated third party bartering. These groups were like banks, where people maintained their accounts. In case of sale of any of the items, the account of the owner would be credited and the account of the buyer would be debited. It is worth mentioning that Adolf Hitler also used barter system to collect money for funding the war. He was engaged in barter trading with Greece, Sweden, and Russia. Post World War II, the people of Germany too resorted to bartering, as the German currency had lost its value. The invention of paper money has lead to an increase in international trade. Today, physical currency is not required, as electronic money is widely used for monetary transactions." (Nair, 2014)

Native peoples used bartering for generation after generation and none of them seemed to die of mass starvation or boredom. Now these more agrarian civilizations were not fabulously wealthy either, but then again their societal models did not call for such things for happiness to exist. Perhaps we are the ones who need to rethink the true values behind a system of total freedom, in order to realize that true freedom actually comes with the duty of spiritual discipline. Before we can acquire, we must first let go--grasping on too tightly to anything, just weakens your grip. The current United States governmental structure is unwilling to make cuts anywhere, or let go of anything, so they will eventually lose everything. All of this is due to greed and their control freak tendencies. As fate would have it, tough times usually do create a more spiritually centered and sane version of society. Hopefully the new version of America is a beautiful sight to behold. Job markets to look to during an economic reset

Other industries that might become popular include sustainable banking, horticulture, communications, bounty hunting, the performing arts (to provide hope), localized delivery services, localized Internet (if the current Internet 2.0 is shutdown), animal husbandry, and many more. Some possible unique businesses ideas include:

-Pressing local non-duplicate able local currencies, or operating a small smelting operation that breaks precious metals down into useful denominations.

-Seed dispensaries for small sustainable vegetable gardens wouldn't be a bad idea,

-Public works employment agencies to put people back to work in a "new deal" fashion.

-Teaching classes on foraging, or perhaps shelter construction, for the underprivileged.

-Small local Internet companies, that prevent mass control, but still facilitate commerce, and communications.

-Establishing local trade markets

- Building a business that provides a service or product

- Creating a likeminded community that shares your passion

-Finding ways to re-purpose the glut of empty commercial real estate that may be languishing and dilapidating.

- Learn sound principles of investing in companies or real estate, skills that can allow you take advantage of what many say will be the greatest buying opportunity the world has ever seen.

Something resembling the Roosevelt's "new deal" might come back into play, this time more on the local government level where small cities work together to put people back to work. In such case we should prepare a 30-40% unemployment rate, during a total economic reorientation. Hopefully it won't be a controlled collapse, but even if there are headless zombies running around the streets, never fear! Life will always provide a way for the good moral people to rise amongst society. A way will always exist, allowing human beings to live in harmony within them, and within society at large. Economic harmony is the rule not the exception.

The world was not founded upon principals of chaos. One quick look around a local construction site, should tell you that America was built upon hard work. As far as I can tell the tree's and the plants don't' take days off. For what would they do if not start to die? Yet the more money hungry people within our species dream of having enough cash to take the rest of their lives off. (Well are they in for a little surprise!) People are retiring earlier and earlier, 30-35 even. How can someone stop working after they have only lived a third of their lives? These are the issues facing the modern trust fund elites worldwide, and it's why they will go to ever lower and more depraved behavior to get their kicks. This is how you might act if you had committed spiritual suicide, a sad state that consumes many more souls than you would think. This is why the collapse will be such a blessing in disguise, as it will expose some of these evil creatures and hopefully allow the good of society to reboot the economic system while.

Whatever form, the Global Economic Reset takes, there will always be those people within society determined to make things work whatever the cost. Some people will be motivated by fear, others by children to feed, yet others will want to see their higher spiritual values become manifest in the outside world. I highly doubt that society is ready for any type of truly communal or egalitarian economic model, so currencies will inevitably still be needed as means of exchange. Although for those who are interested in such postmodern utopist scenarios, a wealth of information can be found here:

(http://en.wikipedia.org/wiki/Post-scarcity_economy)

In real terms, when it comes down to do-or-die, most people step it up a few notches to make things happen. Doom and gloom thinking isn't the solution. Such thinking keeps you rooted in a future that hasn't arrived, or in a past that does not exist. It is only through careful forethought within the present that we make ourselves useful to our community, and to our families and friends. That way, when the time does come, everyone is able to band together without the help of big daddy government.

No one with their head screwed on straight would want a government filled with looters, and murderers to come door to door, and claim to fix problems for us. In fact if a major collapse happens it will be one of the best things that ever happened in this country, as the government will be vulnerable to true ideological attack. And of the decedent gluttony of the general populace will perhaps be put back in check for a time. Hopefully it leads to America reinventing its spiritual identity.

Every cycle has its beginning, and every cycle has its end. Time is only what we make of it. The Federal Reserve had its day in the sun for the last 100 years, a chapter that is soon to close, allowing a new age to take shape! There are a million and one ways to generate income, and create value within society--the only limits are those of our imagination. No one respects a beggar who has an able mind and able body to go out and create value within the world, but chooses to do nothing. So why do we respect a government that does the same? The government is looking for handouts, but needs to get a job!

Sustainable development is merely development that is more in tune with life itself and nature in general. Creating more natural versions of society is simpler than you may think. It really deals more with eliminating the non-essential extraneous distractions from our lives... Now everyone has their own interpretation of what they would call the extraneous activities of society, but we can be sure that the self-delusion of drugs would be high on most people's list to get the boot long-term. The self-delusion humanity face is on the rise, and sanity is in decline. People are finding it harder and harder to define the meaning of their own existence-- and the psychic pressure to conform, breeds the mass psychosis we see today.

11 The New America

As it stands now, America will eventually have to face the music and start over from scratch, insanity breed's instability; and unfortunately the financial machinations in America are cu-cu for coco puffs. Again nature, and the non-manmade world, is perpetually trying to steer things back towards balance and sanity. It's up to us to hear the subtle subconscious voice within ourselves that allows us to reconnect with the higher forms of order within the universe. The new America will inevitably end up going through some form of mass systemic overhaul. This will quite possibly affect all areas of our lives. Just as the enlightenment-changed Europe forever, with schools and works of art springing up everywhere--so too shall America be forced to shift. Think about how much things have changed just since the turn of the century. This can give us some clues towards the type of psychological, and external recapitulation that is upon us. America must give credit, where credit is due. As a country we are only just now living through our adolescent years, and this involves us slowly maturing into adulthood so to speak. The teenage punk dye-your-hair-green phase can only last for so long before someone goes to jail or gets hurt. As the economic collapse deepens, Americans will collectively begin to realize that even freedom has its limits, and the fact that true freedom lies firmly rooted in spiritual discipline. A morally disciplined set of leaders, combined with a mature, and emotionally balanced populace is the only way to sustain prosperity long-term. Evil begets evil, malice begets malice, and so we are only reaping what the banking cabal has sown. If the people lead, the leaders will follow. Subconsciously the entire population, no matter how many drugs they might be on, knows that things are far from harmonious in the United States. This well evidenced by the skyrocketing divorce rates, rampant drug abuse, dropping test scores, rising unemployment, skyrocketing suicide rates, and mass-diagnosis of psychological illnesses. Sadly these are only a few of the major outward markers, pointing towards larger existential problems within our nation. Eric Fromm is one of the foremost thinkers within these spheres of existential development within human psychology, and he has this about to say the subject....

"The sick individual finds himself at home with all other similarly sick individuals. The whole culture is geared to this kind of pathology. The result is that the average individual does not experience the separateness and isolation the fully schizophrenic person feels. He feels at ease among those who suffer from the same deformation; in fact, it is the fully sane person who feels

isolated in the insane society — and he may suffer so much from the incapacity to communicate that it is he who may become psychotic." - (Fromm, 1973)

The silence and acquiescence of the general populace, is a form of existential consent to this behavior, and makes us partially liable for the insanity of those at the top of the totalitarian chain. Again this does not mean that people should be out marching in the streets, conversely these types of actions are generally counterproductive. This same outwardly projected energy could be much more valuably harnessed by working on building character within. When we are able to release the cycles of fear and trauma manifested by the media, and peer groups, we do the subconscious of humanity a great service. It is also beneficial for people to be working towards self-employment, or at least acquiring education towards a more productive occupation for ourselves. Occupations that are independent of the current governmental structure, will obviously be more productive as well. Everyone needs something that they can be passionate about. There is no harm in trying your hand at many different types of work as well, as long as you are learning something valuable about yourself or the larger world around you. Robert Kiyosaki delivered one of my favorite fiscal philosophies of all time in the massively popular Rich Dad Poor Dad series of books.

"I am concerned that too many people are focused too much on money and not on their greatest wealth, which is their education. If people are prepared to be flexible, keep an open mind and learn, they will grow richer and richer through the changes. If they think money will solve the problems, I am afraid those people will have a rough ride. Intelligence solves problems and produces money. Money without financial intelligence is money soon gone." (Kiyosaki, 2011)

Without a long-term vision and a good amount of patience our efforts as individuals won't amount to much. You need to be comfortable with the fact that your personal career, and life goals may take years, or decades to realize—so be ok with that. Cycles of time are there for just such purposes, great deeds require great efforts, and great efforts require patience. The new America will again be cultivated upon such principals, as it was in its inception. The advent of the get rich quick business model, and the permanent decadent vacation lifestyle, has brought this country to the edge of ruin. To make your living at the cost of others prosperity is not something to be proud of. Everyone has the right to material wealth, but in no way does this condone enslaving others to reach said objectives.

The Checklist to Freedom

There is a long laundry list of things that must be done in order to reclaim some fiscal sanity. Current solutions proposed by the political establishment don't seem to address the root issues of the problem. One of the most virulent leaders towards economic reform is Libertarian staple Ron Paul. Along with his son Rand Paul, former congressman Paul has advocated for the abolition of the Federal Reserve, in favor of giving the Federal Reserve's power to issue currency back to the United States government. In effect this would solve the problem of the billions of dollars we pay in interest to the Federal Reserve, but it would still give the sociopathic wackos in Washington way too much power of control over the currency. That's like deposing one dictator, and promoting another. Any long term viable economic solutions from this country are going to need to be either highly decentralized, or under intense public scrutiny 24 hours a day 7 days a week.

The economic To-Do list goes a little something like this:

A. Reclaim America's good name as a bastion of freedom, instead of as a bastion for banker market manipulation. Support Constitutional candidates who will take a stand against the Department of Homeland Security, America's new standing army, the NSA, the TSA, and the police state in general.

B. Abolish the Federal Reserve and IRS. Decentralize the currency into a basket of more regionalized currencies. Thereby creating more competition on an interstate level for businesses, and the lifting of oppressive tax laws. Making this a states' rights or regional issue helps prevent such a concentration of power from occurring again.

C. Open the ledgers of the United States budgets to the common man; every last penny spent by the government should be available to an online QuickBooks account for every taxpayer to see. This will cut out all the drug dealing and insane black budget, N.S.A., and defense projects that serve to further enslave us with our own capital.

D. Make currency policy a states right issue so that currencies are less likely to be co-opted, due to a fear of flight of major industry from that state if things get too out of hand. This could be done in the way of a precious metal backing, crypto currency, barter, or a mixture of these methodologies.

E. Legalize free trade within the United States, and reapply tariffs to imports as has commonly been done throughout history to normalize trade deficits--or prevent them from occurring in the first place. This will also give incentive to keep jobs within the United States, instead of losing them abroad. Also abolish all current so called free trade deals like NAFTA and replace them with true free market principles of allowing businesses to trade internationally without government over regulation.

F. Close tax loopholes for the ultra-rich and multinational corporations wherever possible, it has been documented time, and time again that the ultra rich pay no taxes, and generally speaking steal taxpayer funds through their no bid contracts. Without addressing this elephant in the room, nothing is going to change for too long. We might see the banking manipulation of the markets go into hiding for a good while, but unless controls are put in place to prevent such activities, then nothing will be sustainable.

G. Switching to a flat tax, and obviously abolishing the income tax, while drastically lowering taxes across the board.

H. Ultimately the America of the future should be mostly concerned with the personal liberty of the citizenry, and national defense. Other than that close the military bases around the globe and bring our troops home.

I. The decriminalization of drugs, and the adoption of more effective treatment modalities. I think that everyone can agree AA is a 50/50 cure at best. America needs to wake up and get real about drug abuse, and figure out alternative methods to fixing this national problem. As it stands 1 in 5 adults is on some form of psychiatric drug, (http://www.foxnews.com/health/2011/11/17/one-in-five-american-adults-takes-psychiatric-drugs/and) and another 7-25% depending on the poll smoke week regularly. With 50% of the country living in some form of alternate reality, how are we supposed to get things back on track? This isn't even taking into account the alcohol abuse in our country, which affects one in twelve. America as a whole is running away from their problems in the form of addiction, this needs to be addressed in some fashion. Decriminalizing drug use in America will also lead to the banksters losing their highly profitable drug trade stream of income that has come at the expense of destroying whole communities.

J. Developing systems of alternative healing to deal with the psychological insanity, and healing the deeper issues of people is a must. The western medicine method of applying band-aids, has caused untold death and unhappiness amongst our world. Eastern societies live much longer lives, and are much more emotionally balanced due to these medicinal practices. Instead of placing a focus on death care let us focus on real healthcare issues. The banning of GMO's, fluoride in the water, and the use of dangerous vaccines, chemical additives to our food supply are a must in order to raise up a future generation of critical thinkers.

K. Starting new types of schools that focus on different types of trade skills, as well as bringing educational standards up to par with international norms. We also must bring natural lighting back into schools, fluorescent lighting is killing people's intellect, and causing much of the ADD phenomenon. Rid our schools of common core federal government standardized testing as well as the wicked teachers unions who put tenure ahead of our children's education. Abolish the

Department of education and allow states the control over their public schools. End government backed college loans and replace them with private lending for aspiring college students based on high school success and the possibility of future repayment.

L. Put a tax on television watching. People should have to pay if they want to enjoy their servitude (Ok so maybe were reaching here.) However society must come up with a way to disincentive America's addiction to watching five to six hours of T.V. a day.

M. Teach kids about entrepreneurship and saving money early. In China this is the norm, every child is taught about saving money from when they are 5 years old. In America, only those from the banking caste, or wealthy classes are taught such common sense lessons. In America we teach kids how to be gluttonous consumers. Personal growth icons like Napoleon Hill and Jim Rohn should be required reading in order to pave the way for a renaissance of individual growth and critical thinking.

N. Fixing the food supply. Unless we get rid of the chemtrails and the GMO's nothing is going to change with the health of America. We have pretty much proved the destructiveness of such terrible dietary choices with the skyrocketing cancer rates.

O. Allow only legal immigration to America of highly skilled foreigners as currently implemented in Switzerland.

P. Teaching children about entrepreneurship, unless we do this, we are doomed to most people selling their souls over to companies that are insensitive to their needs and true spiritual talents. Unless America gets off its ass and starts creating things again, economics will continue to stagnate. This goes hand in hand with developing true artisanship, and individuation.

Libertarian policies will definitely not solve all of the economic woes in our country, but they will go a long way in getting the monkey off our back politically-- inspiring the common individual to open up his or her own fledgling small business or the opportunity of higher paying jobs. A sense of community, mixed with the great abundance of food and natural resources that still abound within the United States should make it someone easy to climb out of another big depression. The Internet will also play a key role in shaping things up and cutting costs. The call should go out for everybody to educate those around them, or at least to those who are receptive to such information. This way a sufficient support network can be created, helping people weather the storm during times of major upheaval.

This will not be the last chapter of the United States, as we have too many great minds among us to let an event like this take down the whole country. Suffering may be a part of the transition, but the suffering is only an outgrowth of that which was un-natural to begin with. Again it comes back to becoming very comfortable with change—as well as becoming comfortable with our darker emotions. If we can do that, the path to future prosperity and sanity, are not far off.

Although America is still the greatest country on earth in my opinion, it also has the darkest side of any country as well. Just as Germany had a vicious dark side after its rise to prominence post World War One. Political leaders are merely the physical manifestation of the dark repressed psychic content of the populace. No dictator could ever come to power, in a psychologically healthy, vibrant, artistic, and emotionally balanced society. Sadly every such societal model that exhibited these traits has been wiped off the face of the earth, in a genocidal quest that spans eons.

To regard a global recapitalization as a small undertaking is a grave mistake, but inherently within any set of changes lies growth opportunities. Our own personal healing work and self-cultivation will pay out dividends during tough times. Associating with people of merit who are also living in reality, assures that we can remain at peace with ourselves during any change. No inept leaders, or political parties, or central bankers can decide fate. Fate makes its own decisions, and how we rise above it, or turn to meet it, is up to us. Today is the best time we have ever had to make the long-term changes we have always wanted to make. So in closing, I want to leave you with some words of wisdom from the great sage Lao Tzu. We should do as the Tao Te Ching advises:

"Tackle the difficult when it is easy. Handle the big when it is small. Difficult things beneath heaven Are made up of easy things. Big things beneath heaven Are made up of small things. Thus the sage Never deals with the great, But accomplishes greatness." Tao Te Ching

About Fabian Calvo

Fabian Calvo is one of the leading entrepreneur and real estate investing experts in the world. He has closed thousands of real estate transactions and tens of millions in purchases and sales in over 30 markets in the United States. He is also a recognized economic trends forecaster, political analyst and entrepreneur coach. Fabian is the founder and President of the real estate investment firm "The Note House", creator of the world renowned "Resourceful Real Estate Academy" and "Resourceful Entrepreneur Academy".

His motivation and driving beliefs are founded on the notion that anyone, anywhere, regardless of their current economic condition can achieve financial independence implementing his strategies and tactics. When he began his career over a decade ago, he did not set out to become the world recognized entrepreneur teacher he is today, but when he realized that the corporate elite and Washington bureaucrats want Americans dependent on big government instead of themselves, he knew he had to reveal to the world the investing secrets and strategies used by hedge funds, top online marketers and other top real estate investors so that the average American could also become wealthy and financially free. To date, Fabians programs have sold all over the world and every day he hears from people about how his programs and live events have changed their life.

Fabian has been an active political analyst and commentator for years. In 2006 he hosted a radio show in the greater Tampa Bay Area. In 2007 he was a precinct captain for the Ron Paul campaign and in 2010 he ran for the Florida State House of Representatives. Fabians campaign gave Floridians the option of a true constitutional champion and political outsider.

Fabian Calvo is also recognized around the world as Fabian4Liberty and hosts "The Fabian Calvo Podcast" and the Fabian4Liberty YouTube channel which has over 38,000 subscribers and growing. His videos have over 7 million views globally. He is committed to promoting the principles of our Constitutional Republic and economic liberty as well as exposing the corrupted New World Order political establishment. Education and awareness is the only way Fabian believes we can defeat the criminal elite from taking our liberties. Fabians unparalleled stand against the Federal Reserve & Americas foreign resource wars have made him an alternative go to voice in the age of a lying and dying dinosaur mainstream media.

Works Cited

Abbey, C. (2013, 9 9). Daily Kos. Retrieved 2013, from Daily Kos:

http://www.dailykos.com/story/2013/09/09/1237500/-The-

PetroDollar-Why-Syria#

Berman, M. (2014). Wordpress. Retrieved 2014, from Wordpress:

http://riversong.wordpress.com/civil-war-the-conquest-of-agrarianism-

by-industrialism/

Bloomberg. (2012, February 20). Retrieved 2014, from Bloomberg:

http://www.bloomberg.com/news/2012-02-20/icelandic-anger-brings-

record-debt-relief-in-best-crisis-recovery-story.html

Bloomberg. (2013, September 6). Retrieved 2014, from Bloomberg:

(http://www.bloomberg.com/news/2013-09-06/smithfield-receives-u-s-

regulator-approval-for-shuanghui-deal.html)

Business Time. (2011, August 22). Retrieved 2014, from Business Time:

(http://business.time.com/2011/08/22/has-america-become-a-nation-

of-squatters/#ixzz2qhsLzF00)

Cohen, B. (2014, May). Polsci. UCSB. Retrieved from

(http://www.polsci.ucsb.edu/faculty/cohen/inpress/bretton.html)

Crazy Emails and Back Stories. (2012, May 12). Retrieved 2014, from Crazy Emails and Back Stories:

(=http://crazyemailsandbackstories.wordpress.com/2012/05/12/iceland s-amazing-peaceful-revolution-still-not-in-the-news-backstory/)

Daily Kos. (2011, August 1). Retrieved 2014, from Daily Kos:

http://www.dailykos.com/story/2011/08/01/1001662/-Iceland-s-On-going-Revolution

Demonocracy. (2014). Retrieved from Demonocracy:

(http://demonocracy.info/infographics/usa/us_debt/us_debt.html)

Dr. Ezra Pound. (1950). Washington, DC, USA.

Duman, C. (2014). New York Times. Retrieved 2014, from New York Times.

Eichengreen, B. (2014, May). New York Times. Retrieved 2014, from

http://online.wsj.com/news/articles/SB10001424052748703313304576 132170181013248

Environmental Graffiti. (2014). Retrieved 2014, from Environmental Graffiti: http://www.environmentalgraffiti.com/art-and-design/news-beijings-underground-city

Examiner. (2014). Retrieved 2014, from Examiner:

http://www.examiner.com/article/nations-using-gold-to-purchase-oil-

as-world-begins-to-move-away-from-dollar

Ferrara, P. (2013, March 1). Forbes. Retrieved 2014, from Forbes:

(http://www.forbes.com/sites/peterferrara/2013/03/01/rethinking-

money-the-rise-of-hayeks-private-competing-currencies/)

Flannery, R. (2014). Retrieved from www.forbes.com

Fox Business. (2014, January 16). Retrieved 2014, from Fox Business:

http://www.foxbusiness.com/economy-policy/2014/01/16/china-now-

owns-record-1317t-us-government-debt/

Freedom Outpost. (2013, November). Retrieved 2014, from Freedom

Outpost: (http://freedomoutpost.com/2013/11/russia-and-china-nuke-

the-us/#LrvHlWW6gXSorXMW.99)

Fromm, E. (1973). The Anatomy of Human Destructiveness.

Gavin, A. (2014). Marshall The U.S. Strategy to Control Middle Eastern

Oil. In A. Gavin.

Geo Political Monitor. (2014, May). Retrieved from

http://www.geopoliticalmonitor.com

Gertz, B. (2014). Washington Free Beacon. Retrieved 2014, from

Washington Free Beacon: http://freebeacon.com/guess-whos-coming-

to-dinner-3/

Green, B. (2013, December 24). Business Week. Retrieved 2014, from

Business Week: http://www.businessweek.com/articles/2013-12-

24/the-dollar-will-never-fall-to-bitcoin

Guess, A. (2007, September 27). Inside Highered. Retrieved 2014, from

Inside Highered:

(http://www.insidehighered.com/news/2007/09/27/endowments#ixzz2

rdiwQsYK)

History Learning Site. (2014). Retrieved 2014, from History Learning

Site:

http://www.historylearningsite.co.uk/Roman_Catholic_Church_in_1500

.htm

Info Wars. (2014, May). Retrieved 2014, from Info Wars:

http://www.infowars.com/dont-worry-the-government-says-that-the-

inflation-you-see-is-just-your-imagination/

Investopia. (2014, May). Retrieved 2014, from Investopia:

http://www.investopedia.com/ask/answers/12/derivative.asp

Jackson, A. (1832, July 2). Vetoing the Bank of the United States Veto

Message Regarding the Bank of the United States .

Kiyosaki, R. T. (2011). Rich Dad, Poor Dad.

Lague, D. (2014). Reuters. Retrieved 2014, from Reuters:

http://www.reuters.com/investigates/china-military/

Lincoln, A. (2014). Brainy Quote. Retrieved 2014, from Brainy Quote:

http://www.brainyquote.com/quotes/quotes/a/abrahamlin143183.htm

l#RYF7yAiB1vbUhIzD.99

Mauer, H. (1985). Early Women Masters. Retrieved 2014, from Early

Women Masters: http://earlywomenmasters.net/tao/ch_63.html)

Mckillop, A. (2014, May). Market Oracle. Retrieved from

http://www.marketoracle.co.uk/Article42847.html

Nair, S. (2014). Buzzle. Retrieved 2014, from Buzzle:

http://www.buzzle.com/articles/barter-services-history-of-barter-

system.html)

National Priorities. (2014, May). Retrieved 2014, from National

Priorities: http://nationalpriorities.org/cost-of/

New Advent. (2014, May). Retrieved from

http://www.newadvent.org/cathen/15235c.htm

Oil Control. (2014). Retrieved 2014, from Oil Control:

http://oilcontrol.tripod.com

PBS. (2014). Retrieved 2014, from PBS:

http://www.pbs.org/wgbh/pages/frontline/shows/heroin/etc/history.ht

ml

Postman, N. Amusing Ourselves to Death: Public Discourse in the Age of

Show Business.

Postman, N. Amusing Ourselves to Death.

Sanati, C. (2009, November 12). New York Times. Retrieved from

http://dealbook.nytimes.com/2009/11/12/10-years-later-looking-at-

repeal-of-glass-steagall/?_php=true&_type=blogs&_r=0)

Schiff, P. (2014). Global Research. Retrieved 2014, from Global

Research: (http://www.globalresearch.ca/u-s-dollar-collapse-where-is-

germanys-gold/5321894)

Schuman, M. (n.d.). Time Magazine .

Slate. (2013, October). Retrieved 2014, from Slate:

http://www.slate.com/articles/news_and_politics/foreigners/2013/10/

mauner_mahecha_s_drug_submarines_inside_a_high_tech_south_ame

rican_narco.html)

Snyder, M. (2014, May). The Economic Collapse Blog. Retrieved 2014,

from http://theeconomiccollapseblog.com/archives/the-growing-rift-

with-saudi-arabia-threatens-to-severely-damage-the-petrodollar)

Sutto, A. (2014, May). Third World Traveler. Retrieved from

http://www.thirdworldtraveler.com/Fascism/Wall_Street_Rise_Hitler.ht

ml

Tamney, J. (2012, August). Forbes . Retrieved 2014, from Forbes:

(http://www.forbes.com/sites/johntamny/2012/08/06/are-ron-pauls-

competing-currencies-the-answer-to-monetary-mischief/)

The Matrix (1999). [Motion Picture].

The Money Masters. (2014, May). Retrieved from

http://www.themoneymasters.com/monetary-reform-act/the-five-

"bank-wars"/

Tzu, S. (1792). The Art of War.

Wall Street Journal. (2014). Retrieved from Wall Street Journal:

http://online.wsj.com/news/articles/SB10001424127887324787004578

495250424727708

Wall Street Journal. (2014). Retrieved 2014, from Wall Street Journal:

http://online.wsj.com/news/articles/SB10001424052702304419104579

326701752873782?mg=reno64-

wsj&url=http%3A%2F%2Fonline.wsj.com%2Farticle%2FSB10001424052

702304419104579326701752873782.html

Watkins, T. (2014, May). SJSU EDU. Retrieved 2014, from SJSU EDU:

http://www.sjsu.edu/faculty/watkins/hyper.htm#YUGO

Watson, P. J. (2014, May). Info Wars. Retrieved 2014, from Info Wars:

http://www. Infowars.com

Wikipedia. (2014, May). Retrieved from Wikipedia:

(http://en.wikipedia.org/wiki/Strategic_Petroleum_Reserve_(United_St

ates))

Wikipedia. (2014). Retrieved 2014, from Wikipedia:

(http://en.wikipedia.org/wiki/Nixon_Shock)

Xinhau. (2013, October 14). LA Times. Retrieved 2014, from LA Times: http://articles.latimes.com/2013/oct/14/business/la-fi-shutdown-china-20131015

Zero Hedge. (n.d.). Retrieved 2014, from http://www.zerohedge.com

Zero Hedge. (2014, May).

Abbey, C. (2013, 9 9). Daily Kos. Retrieved 2014, from Daily Kos: http://www.dailykos.com/story/2013/09/09/1237500/-The-PetroDollar-Why-Syria#

Berman, M. (2014). Wordpress. Retrieved 2014, from Wordpress: http://riversong.wordpress.com/civil-war-the-conquest-of-agrarianism-by-industrialism/

Bloomberg. (2012, February 20). Retrieved 2014, from Bloomberg: http://www.bloomberg.com/news/2012-02-20/icelandic-anger-brings-record-debt-relief-in-best-crisis-recovery-story.html

Bloomberg. (2013, September 6). Retrieved 2014, from Bloomberg: (http://www.bloomberg.com/news/2013-09-06/smithfield-receives-u-s-regulator-approval-for-shuanghui-deal.html)

Business Time. (2011, August 22). Retrieved 2014, from Business Time:

(http://business.time.com/2011/08/22/has-america-become-a-nation-

of-squatters/#ixzz2qhsLzF00)

Cohen, B. (2014, May). Polsci. UCSB. Retrieved from

(http://www.polsci.ucsb.edu/faculty/cohen/inpress/bretton.html)

Crazy Emails and Back Stories. (2012, May 12). Retrieved May 2014,

from Crazy Emails and Back Stories:

(=http://crazyemailsandbackstories.wordpress.com/2012/05/12/iceland

s-amazing-peaceful-revolution-still-not-in-the-news-backstory/)

Daily Kos. (2011, August 1). Retrieved 2014, from Daily Kos:

http://www.dailykos.com/story/2011/08/01/1001662/-Iceland-s-On-

going-Revolution

Demonocracy. (2014). Retrieved from Demonocracy:

(http://demonocracy.info/infographics/usa/us_debt/us_debt.html)

Dr. Ezra Pound. (1950). Washington, DC, USA.

Duman, C. (2014). New York Times. Retrieved 2014, from New York

Times.

Eichengreen, B. (2014, May). New York Times. Retrieved 2014, from

http://online.wsj.com/news/articles/SB1000142405274870331330457

6132170181013248

Environmental Graffiti. (2014). Retrieved 2014, from Environmental

Graffiti: http://www.environmentalgraffiti.com/art-and-design/news-

beijings-underground-city

Examiner. (2014). Retrieved 2014, from Examiner:

http://www.examiner.com/article/nations-using-gold-to-purchase-oil-

as-world-begins-to-move-away-from-dollar

Ferrara, P. (2013, March 1). Forbes. Retrieved 2014, from Forbes:

(http://www.forbes.com/sltes/peterferrara/2013/03/01/rethinking-

money-the-rise-of-hayeks-private-competing-currencies/)

Flannery, R. (2014). Retrieved from www.forbes.com

Fox Business. (2014, January 16). Retrieved 2014, from Fox Business:

http://www.foxbusiness.com/economy-policy/2014/01/16/china-now-

owns-record-1317t-us-government-debt/

Freedom Outpost. (2013, November). Retrieved 2014, from Freedom

Outpost: (http://freedomoutpost.com/2013/11/russia-and-china-nuke-

the-us/#LrvHlWW6gXSorXMW.99)

Fromm, E. (1973). The Anatomy of Human Destructiveness.

Gavin, A. (2014). Marshall The U.S. Strategy to Control Middle Eastern

Oil. In A. Gavin.

Geo Political Monitor. (2014, May). Retrieved from

http://www.geopoliticalmonitor.com

Gertz, B. (2014). Washington Free Beacon. Retrieved 2014, from

Washington Free Beacon: http://freebeacon.com/guess-whos-coming-

to-dinner-3/

Green, B. (2013, December 24). Business Week. Retrieved 2014, from

Business Week: http://www.businessweek.com/articles/2013-12-

24/the-dollar-will-never-fall-to-bitcoin

Guess, A. (2007, September 27). Inside Highered. Retrieved 2014, from

Inside Highered:

(http://www.insidehighered.com/news/2007/09/27/endowments#ixzz2

rdiwQsYK)

History Learning Site. (2014). Retrieved 2014, from History Learning

Site:

http://www.historylearningsite.co.uk/Roman_Catholic_Church_in_1500

.htm

Info Wars. (2014, May). Retrieved 2014, from Info Wars:

http://www.infowars.com/dont-worry-the-government-says-that-the-

inflation-you-see-is-just-your-imagination/

Investopia. (2014, May). Retrieved 2014, from Investopia:

http://www.investopedia.com/ask/answers/12/derivative.asp

Jackson, A. (1832, July 2). Vetoing the Bank of the United States Veto

Message Regarding the Bank of the United States .

Kiyosaki, R. T. (2011). Rich Dad, Poor Dad.

Lague, D. (2014). Reuters. Retrieved 2014, from Reuters:

http://www.reuters.com/investigates/china-military/

Lincoln, A. (2014). Brainy Quote. Retrieved 2014, from Brainy Quote:

http://www.brainyquote.com/quotes/quotes/a/abrahamlin143183.htm

l#RYF7yAiB1vbUhIzD.99

Mauer, H. (1985). Early Women Masters. Retrieved 2014, from Early Women Masters: http://earlywomenmasters.net/tao/ch_63.html)

Mckillop, A. (2014, May). Market Oracle. Retrieved from http://www.marketoracle.co.uk/Article42847.html

Nair, S. (2014). Buzzle. Retrieved 2014, from Buzzle: http://www.buzzle.com/articles/barter-services-history-of-barter-system.html)

National Priorities. (2014, May). Retrieved 2014, from National Priorities: http://nationalpriorities.org/cost-of/

New Advent. (2014, May). Retrieved from http://www.newadvent.org/cathen/15235c.htm

Oil Control. (2014). Retrieved 2014, from Oil Control: http://oilcontrol.tripod.com

PBS. (2014). Retrieved 2014, from PBS: http://www.pbs.org/wgbh/pages/frontline/shows/heroin/etc/history.html

Postman, N. Amusing Ourselves to Death: Public Discourse in the Age of Show Business.

Postman, N. Amusing Ourselves to Death.

Sanati, C. (2009, November 12). New York Times. Retrieved from

http://dealbook.nytimes.com/2009/11/12/10-years-later-looking-at-

repeal-of-glass-steagall/?_php=true&_type=blogs&_r=0)

Schiff, P. (2014). Global Research. Retrieved 2014, from Global

Research: (http://www.globalresearch.ca/u-s-dollar-collapse-where-is-

germanys-gold/5321894)

Schuman, M. (n.d.). Time Magazine .

Slate. (2013, October). Retrieved 2014, from Slate:

http://www.slate.com/articles/news_and_politics/foreigners/2013/10/

mauner_mahecha_s_drug_submarines_inside_a_high_tech_south_ame

rican_narco.html)

Snyder, M. (2014, May). The Economic Collapse Blog. Retrieved 2014,

from http://theeconomiccollapseblog.com/archives/the-growing-rift-

with-saudi-arabia-threatens-to-severely-damage-the-petrodollar)

Sutto, A. (2014, May). Third World Traveler. Retrieved from

http://www.thirdworldtraveler.com/Fascism/Wall_Street_Rise_Hitler.ht

ml

Tamney, J. (2012, August). Forbes . Retrieved 2014, from Forbes:

(http://www.forbes.com/sites/johntamny/2012/08/06/are-ron-pauls-

competing-currencies-the-answer-to-monetary-mischief/)

The Matrix (1999). [Motion Picture].

The Money Masters. (2014, May). Retrieved from

http://www.themoneymasters.com/monetary-reform-act/the-five-

"bank-wars"/

Tzu, S. (1792). The Art of War.

Wall Street Journal. (2014). Retrieved from Wall Street Journal:

http://online.wsj.com/news/articles/SB10001424127887324787004578

495250424727708

Wall Street Journal. (2014). Retrieved 2014, from Wall Street Journal:

http://online.wsj.com/news/articles/SB10001424052702304419104579

326701752873782?mg=reno64-

wsj&url=http%3A%2F%2Fonline.wsj.com%2Farticle%2FSB10001424052

7023044191045793267017528737 82.html

Watkins, T. (2014, May). SJSU EDU. Retrieved May 2014, from SJSU EDU:

http://www.sjsu.edu/faculty/watkins/hyper.htm#YUGO

Watson, P. J. (2014, May). Info Wars. Retrieved May 2014, from Info

Wars: http://www. Infowars.com

Wikipedia. (2014, May). Retrieved from Wikipedia:

(http://en.wikipedia.org/wiki/Strategic_Petroleum_Reserve_(United_St

ates))

Wikipedia. (2014). Retrieved 2014, from Wikipedia:

(http://en.wikipedia.org/wiki/Nixon_Shock)

Xinhau. (2013, October 14). LA Times. Retrieved May 2014, from LA

Times: http://articles.latimes.com/2013/oct/14/business/la-fi-

shutdown-china-20131015

Zero Hedge. (n.d.). Retrieved 2014, from http://www.zerohedge.com

Zero Hedge. (2014, May).